# A
# LETTER
# TO
# ROME

Dr. Oscar C. Johnson PhD

# PREFACE

Over the years I have been fascinated with the Apostle Paul's letter to the Christian Church in Rome. I have read this epistle well over 10 times and am always in awe of the content of the letter. The Lord inspired me to write this book to give the best explanation of the Apostle' Paul's concepts of sin and salvation in prose so that understanding is possible in all but the youngest age group. This is a short book as it only addresses one letter from Paul. However, I think that it is thorough in its explanation of original sin, what one should expect as a result of sin, the justice of God and the means of justification and salvation. To me, it defines everything necessary for someone to understand the condition of their spiritual being, whether one is a born-again Christian or one who is not sure of their standing with God.

The letter to the Romans is a flawless and organized presentation of the Christian doctrine. It begins with the sins of man and the condemnation of man as a result of his sins. This situation is not unlike today. The majority of the people in the world continue to reject the sovereignty of God and rarely consider the effects of their sinfulness. But for the ones who do realize sin is a problem, many do not know what to do to achieve redemption. Of course, the most common alleviation of their predicament is to rationalize that if they are a good person then they will be saved.

Paul's letter makes it clear that this is not the case and that even the good will suffer eternal damnation. But God is merciful and provides a way for redemption. Paul's letter clearly explains how one becomes justified in God's eyes and gains salvation.

This letter is clear on the role of Jesus and the importance of following in his footsteps. Understanding this letter whether Jew or Gentile, Christian or not, one will have to reflect in the logic of the "what if, then" scenario. The letter provides a definite theological foundation on which one can develop their faith and grow in Christ.

I believe a careful evaluation and meditation of this text will change one's life for the better and provides continual improvement in one's spirit as they work to understand the will of God.

# TABLE OF CONTENTS

# INTRODUCTION

The Apostle Paul's letter to Rome appears in the New Testament as the 6th book. It follows the Book of Acts which chronicles what the apostles did after Jesus ascended to Heaven. The author of the Book of Acts was the Apostle Luke who is interesting as he, a Gentile, is one of the 4 Gospel writers, Matthew, Mark, Luke and John. The Book of Acts is somewhat a continuation of the message regarding the ministry of Jesus and his disciples.

To understand some basics, the first 3 books of the Gospels are called the Synoptic gospels. These are similar accounts of the life of Jesus with the points of view from the different authors. The book of John is written with a different perspective. It is more reflective of the life of Jesus and considers His preexistence and full deity.

I clarify the words gospel and synoptic and why the Apostle John's book was different. It is not uncommon for the novice Bible reader, though they may have heard these words, do not really know what they mean. The word "gospel" is translated from the Greek word "evangelion" which means "good news". The gospels of Matthew, Mark, and Luke are collectively called the "Synoptic" gospels based on the Greek word that means "the common view". Though each story is basically the same, each writer has a distinguishing interpretation of Jesus's life and mission. On the other hand, the Apostle John is different approach to writing about Jesus. In his book, he presents Jesus in a more theological setting.

Luke was an intimate friend of Paul and at times was referred to as the "beloved physician". He was different from the other gospel writers because he was a Gentile. Luke and Paul met on Paul's 2nd missionary journey. Luke was highly intelligent and was in fact a physician. He studied under Paul and was left in Philippi during this 2nd mission. He does meet with Paul again during Paul's 3rd missionary journey and traveled with him to Jerusalem and Rome. Luke was with Paul for well over 3 years in this missionary journey. During this missionary journey Paul traveled to Galatia, Corinth, and Ephesus collecting money which he delivered to the poor saints in Jerusalem. In Luke's Book of Acts he details much of Paul's ministry during their travels.

Paul was in Corinth when he wrote the letter to the Roman Christians. This was in the Spring of 58 C.E. It is the longest of his epistles and is the most doctrinally significant. Though he wrote letters to many of the churches he established in many cities, the letter to Rome comprehensively covers critical aspects of Christian theology. It divulges the answers to important questions and provides material evidence on topics of sinful nature of man, salvation, the sovereignty of God, judgment, spiritual growth, and the righteousness of God. It is noticeable that Paul does not discuss the Resurrection, the Eucharist or the End Times prophecies. Paul is fervent in his apologetics (the defense of Christian theology) and his pastoral approach to presenting the righteousness of God that is discernable through HIS Word and HIS son Jesus. Paul had never been to Rome but wanted to assure the Christian Church in Rome that he anticipated seeing them and planned on going to Rome on his was to Spain. This was part of his mission to spread the Gospel of the Kingdom of Heaven.

The person who reads the Letter to Rome will receive answers to critical questions about sin and salvation. Paul makes this very clear. He reminds them that as Jews they had been chosen by God. This was a point of pride among the Hebrew people, but that did not mean they were favored over the Gentiles who accepted Jesus as their savior. Paul declares that righteousness is now obtained through acceptance of Jesus rather than the Mosaic laws of the Old Testament. This is the focus of the letter. The "righteousness of God" is interspersed throughout the whole epistle.

# CHAPTER I

¹**Paul, a bondservant of Jesus Christ, called *to be* an apostle, separated to the gospel of God**

² **which He promised before through His prophets in the Holy Scriptures,**

³ **concerning His Son Jesus Christ our Lord, who [a]was born of the seed of David according to the flesh,**

⁴ ***and* declared *to be* the Son of God with power according to the Spirit of holiness, by the resurrection from the dead.**

⁵ **Through Him we have received grace and apostleship for obedience to the faith among all nations for His name,**

⁶ **among whom you also are the called of Jesus Christ;**

⁷ **To all who are in Rome, beloved of God, called *to be* saints:**

**Grace to you and peace from God our Father and the Lord Jesus Christ. (Romans 1:1-7 NKJV)**

The Book of Paul begins with Paul giving his credentials. First, he wants to explain that he, is before anything else, a servant of Jesus Christ. In the Greek, the word "doulos" actually translates to "bondservant" (Oxford Reference). In the Jewish community it is known that a bondservant is a person who sells themselves into slavery for a period of time or indefinitely. Calling himself a bondservant to Jesus informs the Church that he belongs to Jesus acknowledging him as his Lord and possessor.

Paul was not always called Paul. Before he became a bondservant to Jesus he was known as Saul of Tarsus, a Pharisee of the Jews. Saul was God faring and absolute in his obedience to Mosaic Law. He was considered the Jews, Jew because of his knowledge of Torah and by-laws. Above all, he hated followers of Jesus honestly believing that Jesus was a heretic and blasphemer on a mission to destroy the souls of the God's chosen, the people of Israel. At that time, these followers had no official name but were known as the followers of the Way. Saul wanted to put an end to this wayward divergence from Judaism.

But then things changed.

**¹Then Saul, still breathing threats and murder against the disciples of the Lord, went to the high priest**

**² and asked letters from him to the synagogues of Damascus, so that if he found any who were of the Way, whether men or women, he might bring them bound to Jerusalem.**

**³ As he journeyed, he came near Damascus, and suddenly a light shone around him from heaven.**

**⁴ Then he fell to the ground, and heard a voice saying to him, "Saul, Saul, why are you persecuting Me?"**

**⁵ And he said, "Who are You, Lord?"**
**Then the Lord said, "I am Jesus, whom you are persecuting. [a]It _is_ hard for you to kick against the goads."**

**⁶ So he, trembling and astonished, said, "Lord, what do You want me to do?" (Acts 9:1-6 NKJV)**

At this point Saul had an epiphany and now knew the errors of his ways. It was this point that he became the bondservant of Jesus.

He continues his greeting stating that he was called to be an Apostle.

Merriam/Webster defines the word as,

: one sent on a mission: such as

**a:** one of an authoritative New Testament group sent out to preach the gospel and made up especially of Christ's 12 original disciples and Paul

**b:** the first prominent Christian missionary to a region or group St. Boniface, the *Apostle* of Germany

(Merriam-Webster Dictionary)

As an apostle of Jesus Christ, Paul had the authority to representant Jesus and speak with Jesus's authority. It had already been common knowledge that the 12 disciples of Jesus were apostles. These where Simon knows as Peter, Andrew, James and John, sons of Zebedee, Philip, Bartholomew, Thomas, Matthew the tax collector, James, son of Alphaeus, Thaddeus, Simon the Zealot, and Judas Iscariot who betrayed Jesus. Traditionally, Paul was considered the 13th Apostle.

Paul became an apostle after his encounter with Jesus on the road to Damascus.

**13 Then Ananias answered, "Lord, I have heard from many about this man, how much [b]harm he has done to Your saints in Jerusalem.**

**14 And here he has authority from the chief priests to bind all who call on Your name."**

**15 But the Lord said to him, "Go, for he is a chosen vessel of Mine to bear My name before Gentiles, kings, and the children[c] of Israel.**

**16 For I will show him how many things he must suffer for My name's sake." (Acts 9:13-16 NKJV)**

Saul now converted to believing in Jesus, started to use the name Paul. After some time, teaching and learning from the God and also from the disciples in Damascus, Paul traveled throughout the area preaching. At some point he had a revelation to go to Jerusalem. It is here that he met Joseph, a Levite from Cyprus, whom the apostles called Barnabas (which means 'son of encouragement'), Barnabas was considered a good man. He was trusted and well-liked by the apostles of Jesus. He was known to have led many Jews to the Christian faith in addition to Gentiles also. Though they became friends and Barabas understood his mission, the disciple/apostles of Jesus were less easily convinced. They had heard or his extreme persecution of the followers of Jesus. So on his first visit to Jerusalem, he was not received by the assembly of the apostles of Jesus. and Paul left Jerusalem and started his first missionary journey.

Now the apostles of Jesus in Jerusalem heard of many conversions of many Gentiles in the Hellenistic city of Antioch. They dispatched Barnabas to find out more about the conversions and to assist in any way that he could. Barnabas knew that Paul had been preaching in Asia Minor after leaving Jerusalem and sought to find him to ask if he would help in the Antioch ministry. He found Paul in Tarsus. Barnabas saw that Paul had become a fervent follower of Christ. Barnabas took the then unknown disciple under his tutelage and protection. They began traveling together preaching the Gospel. It was in Antioch while meeting with the governor the term Christian was first coined for the followers of Christ.

13 years later, Barnabas and Paul returned to Jerusalem. There was still consternation to the idea that Paul, the Jews Jew and Pharisee of the Judaizers, should be considered an apostle of Jesus. They were reticent because of Paul's past actions. Barnabas spoke on behalf of Paul and convinced the apostles that Paul truly was sent to speak with the authority of Jesus.

**26 And when Saul had come to Jerusalem, he tried to join the disciples; but they were all afraid of him, and did not believe that he was a disciple.**

**27 But Barnabas took him and brought *him* to the apostles. And he declared to them how he had seen the Lord on the road, and that He had spoken to him, and how he had preached boldly at Damascus in the name of Jesus. (Acts 9-26-27 NKJV)**

**7 But on the contrary, when they saw that the gospel for the uncircumcised had been committed to me, as *the gospel* for the circumcised *was* to Peter**

**8 (for He who worked effectively in Peter for the apostleship to the circumcised also worked effectively in me toward the Gentiles),**

**9 and when James, [c]Cephas, and John, who seemed to be pillars, perceived the grace that had been given to me, they gave me and Barnabas the right hand of fellowship, that we *should go* to the Gentiles and they to the circumcised. (Galatians 2:7-9 NKJV)**

Thus, the apostles accepted the authority and qualifications of Paul as a representative of Jesus, first to Jews but then to the Gentiles. This was at a time when the apostles of Jesus were only proselytizing to the Jews.

Paul concludes his greeting, giving thanks to the Roman Christians for their faith in Jesus. He acknowledges that their faith is known throughout the world. As Paul states, it is his mission to spread the Gospel of Jesus to the whole world.

> **5 Through Him we have received grace and apostleship for obedience to the faith among all nations for His name,**
>
> **6 among whom you also are the called of Jesus Christ; (Romans 1:5-6 NKJV)**

Paul now calls on God to witness what he is about to say to the Church. In this he is proclaiming that anything that he says is truth because God is with him in spirit. Paul wants the Christians to know that he serves God. There should be no doubt that every action of his, every word of his is for the glory and praise of the Lord as he teaches the gospel of Jesus. More importantly, is that to all who hears the Word and accepts Jesus will share in the spirit with God.

> **9 For God is my witness, whom I serve [b]with my spirit in the gospel of His Son, that without ceasing I make mention of you always in my prayers,**
>
> **10 making request if, by some means, now at last I may find a way in the will of God to come to you.**

**11** For I long to see you, that I may impart to you some spiritual gift, so that you may be established—

**12** that is, that I may be encouraged together with you by the mutual faith both of you and me. (Romans 1:9-12 NKJV)

Paul then makes what many call the dominant theme of the Book of Romans.

**16** For I am not ashamed of the gospel [c]of Christ, for it is the power of God to salvation for everyone who believes, for the Jew first and also for the Greek.

**17** For in it the righteousness of God is revealed from faith to faith; as it is written, "The just shall live by faith." (Romans 1:16-17 NKJV)

He tells us that the righteousness of God is revealed in our faith. This faith being in Jesus Christ. "Living by faith" was not a new concept. In this statement Paul recalls the words of the prophet Habakkuk 600 hundred years earlier. Habakkuk states that the gospel of God is "good news" for all humanity.

**4**"Behold the proud,
His soul is not upright in him;
But the just shall live by his faith. (Habakkuk 2:4 NKJV)

He is not ashamed of his commitment to the Gospel of Jesus. He knew the consequences of this commitment could mean imprisonment and torture or possibly death. The message of Jesus was new and strange to many. For thousands of years the Jewish people had believed in one way, the Greeks had their own gods and concept of salvation, the pagan Romans were worshippers of the Sun God, Sol Invictus. There were countless other fringe religions in existence throughout the area and world. To preach the Gospel of Jesus as a new truth was directly calling all the other religions false. Accordingly, inherent risk was associated, especially since Christians were being persecuted.

Nonetheless, a Christians faith must be in Jesus to be justified before God. The Christian must believe that Jesus died on the cross for the sins of man in order to attain salvation. God has made his power known to man and made them aware of their sin from the beginning of creation. This Paul believed was true and that is why he was not ashamed.

For those who refuse to believe will incur the wrath of God. Those who lived in sin would suffer the holy anger of God. Paul wants people to understand how awful sin really is and how much disdain God has for it. He explains that unrighteousness has always been with man. God's truth also has always been with man. The problem is that man does not want to know about the truth. They would rather suppress it to give into their worldly lust. Because of the sinful nature of man, willing choices are made to neglect and ignore the Lord's truths.

**18 For the wrath of God is revealed from heaven against all ungodliness and unrighteousness of men, who [d]suppress the truth in unrighteousness,**

**19 because what may be known of God is [e]manifest [f]in them, for God has shown *it* to them.**

**20 For since the creation of the world His invisible *attributes* are clearly seen, being understood by the things that are made, *even* His eternal power and [g]Godhead, so that they are without excuse,**

²¹ because, although they knew God, they did not glorify *Him* as God, nor were thankful, but became futile in their thoughts, and their foolish hearts were darkened.

²² Professing to be wise, they became fools,

²³ and changed the glory of the incorruptible God into an image made like [h]corruptible man—and birds and four-footed animals and creeping things.

²⁴ Therefore God also gave them up to uncleanness, in the lusts of their hearts, to dishonor their bodies among themselves,

²⁵ who exchanged the truth of God for the lie, and worshiped and served the creature rather than the Creator, who is blessed forever. Amen.

²⁶ For this reason God gave them up to vile passions. For even their [i]women exchanged the natural use for what is against nature.

²⁷ Likewise also the [j]men, leaving the natural use of the [k]woman, burned in their lust for one another, men with men committing what is shameful, and receiving in themselves the penalty of their error which was due.

²⁸ And even as they did not like to retain God in *their* knowledge, God gave them over to a debased mind, to do those things which are not fitting;

²⁹ being filled with all unrighteousness, [l]sexual immorality, wickedness, [m]covetousness, [n.]maliciousness; full of envy, murder, strife, deceit, evil-mindedness; *they are* whisperers,

**30** backbiters, haters of God, violent, proud, boasters, inventors of evil things, disobedient to parents,

**31** [o]undiscerning, untrustworthy, unloving, [p]unforgiving, unmerciful;

**32** who, knowing the righteous judgment of God, that those who practice such things are deserving of death, not only do the same but also approve of those who practice them. (Romans 1:18-32 NKJV)

Those who live in sin and refuse to accept Jesus as their savior will be subject to only one fate. This is death.

# CHAPTER II

¹Therefore you are inexcusable, O man, whoever you are who judge, for in whatever you judge another you condemn yourself; for you who judge practice the same things.

² But we know that the judgment of God is according to truth against those who practice such things.

³ And do you think this, O man, you who judge those practicing such things, and doing the same, that you will escape the judgment of God?

⁴ Or do you despise the riches of His goodness, forbearance, and longsuffering, not knowing that the goodness of God leads you to repentance?

⁵ But in accordance with your hardness and your [a]impenitent heart you are [b]treasuring up for yourself wrath in the day of wrath and revelation of the righteous judgment of God,

⁶ who "will render to each one according to his deeds":

⁷ eternal life to those who by patient continuance in doing good seek for glory, honor, and immortality;

⁸ but to those who are self-seeking and do not obey the truth, but obey unrighteousness—indignation and wrath,

⁹ tribulation and anguish, on every soul of man who does evil, of the Jew first and also of the [c]Greek;

**10** but glory, honor, and peace to everyone who works what is good, to the Jew first and also to the Greek.

**11** For there is no partiality with God.

**12** For as many as have sinned without law will also perish without law, and as many as have sinned in the law will be judged by the law

**13** (for not the hearers of the law *are* just in the sight of God, but the doers of the law will be justified;

**14** for when Gentiles, who do not have the law, by nature do the things in the law, these, although not having the law, are a law to themselves,

**15** who show the work of the law written in their hearts, their conscience also bearing witness, and between themselves *their* thoughts accusing or else excusing *them*)

**16** in the day when God will judge the secrets of men by Jesus Christ, according to my gospel. (Romans 2:1-16 NKJV)

Chapter II is basically a continuation of Chapter I. Paul had explained the things that God abhors. He then points directly at the people in the church who feel that they are above those sins and therefore can judge. They are reminded though that they too are guilty of the sins that they judge others of. People may try and hide their sin, but this is in vain. God knows and will not let those hidden sins go unpunished. Without a doubt all are guilty of some sort of sin, so isn't it righteous to receive judgement? The answer is yes. God is just and must pass judgement on those who sin. The Christian cannot take it upon themselves to Judge for they are being judged by God.

Now the Jewish may think that these sins do not pertain to them. They have the Mosaic Laws to protect. They also know that they are God's chosen people and believe that he would not condemn them for their sins. They could never be so wrong. Jewish people sin. They are born with a sinful nature as with everyone else. Even the most pious are sinners and hypocrites. Jesus makes this point clear.

**¹Then Jesus said to the crowds and to his disciples:**

**² "The teachers of the law and the Pharisees sit in Moses' seat.**

**³ So you must be careful to do everything they tell you. But do not do what they do, for they do not practice what they preach.**

**⁴ They tie up heavy, cumbersome loads and put them on other people's shoulders, but they themselves are not willing to lift a finger to move them.**

**⁵ "Everything they do is done for people to see: They make their phylacteries[a] wide and the tassels on their garments long;**

**⁶ they love the place of honor at banquets and the most important seats in the synagogues;**

**⁷ they love to be greeted with respect in the marketplaces and to be called 'Rabbi' by others. (Matthew 23:1-7 NKJV)**

They should not assume they are immune from God's judgment. He shows no favoritism. Paul has described two types of people. There are those who live under the laws of Moses and those who don't live under the laws of Moses. This means there are Jews and then there is everybody else.

God has instilled a conscious in all people. This gives everyone a sense of right and wrong. Invariably, one will choose sin. If one sins under the law, they will be judged by the law. In the end they will perish. Everybody else not bound by the law will perish also. They will just perish without the law. They become a law unto themselves making decisions based on their own consciousness. On judgement day, all will be judged.

Turning his focus to the Jews, Paul describes how they see themselves. The Jewish people believe that their morality is greater than Gentiles. They believe that they know God's will and have advantage because they are the chosen people of God. He then questions them on their obedience to the law.

The Jewish people feel they are persecuted for their beliefs. That may be partially true. The Jewish are very condescending to the Gentiles because they have the Mosaic Laws. What the Gentiles see is a people who dishonor their God by not living by the laws they so famously claim. It is no small wonder that the Gentiles curse the Jewish God. Paul references Isaiah who spoke of the blasphemes of Gentiles.

**17 [d]Indeed you are called a Jew, and rest[e] on the law, and make your boast in God,**

**18 and know *His* will, and approve the things that are excellent, being instructed out of the law,**
**19 and are confident that you yourself are a guide to the blind, a light to those who are in darkness,**

**20 an instructor of the foolish, a teacher of babes, having the form of knowledge and truth in the law.**

**21** You, therefore, who teach another, do you not teach yourself? You who preach that a man should not steal, do you steal?

**22** You who say, "Do not commit adultery," do you commit adultery? You who abhor idols, do you rob temples?

**23** You who make your boast in the law, do you dishonor God through breaking the law?

**24** For "the name of God is blasphemed among the Gentiles because of you," as it is written. (Romans 2:17-24 NKJV)

Paul wants the Jewish people to know that their confidence is misplaced. Being the chosen people or having the law does not make them immune from God's righteous judgement for their sins. Jews are just as guilty as Gentiles and must be saved by grace for there is no other way.

In the remainder of the chapter Paul discusses a major differentiation between Jews and Gentiles. This is the practice of circumcision. This was an aspect of Jewish life. It dated back to the father of the Israeli people. God instructed Abraham to be circumcised as an act of obedience. This act was to be passed down throughout the ages of the Jewish people.

**9** And God said to Abraham: "As for you, you shall keep My covenant, you and your descendants after you throughout their generations.

**10** This *is* My covenant which you shall keep, between Me and you and your descendants after you: Every male child among you shall be circumcised;

**¹¹ and you shall be circumcised in the flesh of your foreskins, and it shall be a sign of the covenant between Me and you. (Genesis 17:9-11 NKJV)**

Circumcision identified the people of Israel as God's chosen people. It did make the people special, but it does not give them favor with regard to salvation. Yet, the Jewish people believed that they were saved by their circumcision.

Paul, being Jewish understood the importance of circumcision to his people, but he also realized that circumcision was only beneficial if one was obedient to the law. Being disobedient would break the covenant with God and revert one spiritually to an uncircumcised state. He explains that if a Gentile is obedient to the divine law of God that he should be considered circumcised. Paul understands that true circumcision is of the heart not the physical act of cutting the foreskin.

**²⁵ For circumcision is indeed profitable if you keep the law; but if you are a breaker of the law, your circumcision has become uncircumcision.**

**²⁶ Therefore, if an uncircumcised man keeps the righteous requirements of the law, will not his uncircumcision be counted as circumcision?**

**²⁷ And will not the physically uncircumcised, if he fulfills the law, judge you who, *even* with *your* [f]written *code* and circumcision, *are* a transgressor of the law?**

**²⁸ For he is not a Jew who *is one* outwardly, nor *is* circumcision that which *is* outward in the flesh;**

**29 but *he is* a Jew who *is one* inwardly; and circumcision *is that* of the heart, in the Spirit, not in the letter; whose [g]praise *is* not from men but from God. (Romans 2:25-28 NKJV)**

The issue of circumcision became a major issue amongst the Jewish spiritual leadership. The disciples of Jesus had followed a rule that would allow Gentiles to become Christian only if they were circumcised. Paul did not take this position and was in actuality fervently against it and any other Jewish laws that were being imposed on a people that were never exposed to them. The Romans and Greeks also found this untenable (Hodges,2001). This created a controversy that would play a major role in the history of Christianity and Christian theology (Stendahl, 1963).

Paul, with his fellow apostle Barnabas, took his argument to the "Pillars of the Church", James the Just, Peter (also called Cephas) and John "the Apostle that Jesus loved" in Jerusalem (Bokenkotter, 2004). This meeting was later called the Council of Jerusalem. In this meeting the Evangelizing mission of Paul and Barnabas to the Gentiles was legitimized. More important to Paul though was the Gentiles being released from the majority of Mosaic Law (Cross & Livingstone, 2005). In particular was the topic of circumcision.

James, who was the leader of the disciples, interpreted the Great Commission determined that the Church had to follow the laws of Torah (Jacobs, 2012). Paul argued against this position. How could Gentiles be expected to adhere to traditional Judaism when this was not part of their culture. God includes everyone who accepts the message of faith in Jesus for salvation. Jewish tradition is not a factor. Paul maintains that we are not circumcised by a physical act, we are circumcised in the heart. James, after deep consideration, acquiesced and agreed with Paul.

¹While Paul and Barnabas were at Antioch of Syria, some men from Judea arrived and began to teach the believers[a]: "Unless you are circumcised as required by the law of Moses, you cannot be saved."

² Paul and Barnabas disagreed with them, arguing vehemently. Finally, the church decided to send Paul and Barnabas to Jerusalem, accompanied by some local believers, to talk to the apostles and elders about this question.

³ The church sent the delegates to Jerusalem, and they stopped along the way in Phoenicia and Samaria to visit the believers. They told them—much to everyone's joy—that the Gentiles, too, were being converted.

⁴ When they arrived in Jerusalem, Barnabas and Paul were welcomed by the whole church, including the apostles and elders. They reported everything God had done through them.
⁵ But then some of the believers who belonged to the sect of the Pharisees stood up and insisted, "The Gentile converts must be circumcised and required to follow the law of Moses."

⁶ So the apostles and elders met together to resolve this issue.

⁷ At the meeting, after a long discussion, Peter stood and addressed them as follows: "Brothers, you all know that God chose me from among you some time ago to preach to the Gentiles so that they could hear the Good News and believe.

⁸ God knows people's hearts, and he confirmed that he accepts Gentiles by giving them the Holy Spirit, just as he did to us.

**9** He made no distinction between us and them, for he cleansed their hearts through faith.

**10** So why are you now challenging God by burdening the Gentile believers[b] with a yoke that neither we nor our ancestors were able to bear?

**11** We believe that we are all saved the same way, by the undeserved grace of the Lord Jesus."

**12** Everyone listened quietly as Barnabas and Paul told about the miraculous signs and wonders God had done through them among the Gentiles.

**13** When they had finished, James stood and said, "Brothers, listen to me.

**14** Peter[c] has told you about the time God first visited the Gentiles to take from them a people for himself.

**15** And this conversion of Gentiles is exactly what the prophets predicted. As it is written:

**16** Afterward I will return
　and restore the fallen house[d] of David.
　I will rebuild its ruins
　and restore it,

**17** so that the rest of humanity might seek the Lᴏʀᴅ,
　including the Gentiles—
　all those I have called to be mine.

The Lᴏʀᴅ has spoken—

**18** he who made these things known so long ago.'[e]

<sup>19</sup> "And so my judgment is that we should not make it difficult for the Gentiles who are turning to God. (Acts 15:1-19 NKJV)

# CHAPTER III

Paul begins this chapter with rhetorical questions. Is there an advantage to being a Jew? Is it an advantage to be circumcised? Is the faithfulness of Gentiles to God without recognition? God's judgement is defended.

God will recognize those who are faithful to him whether they are followers of Judaism or not. As a nation, the Jewish are advantaged since they were given the "Word" from God. Still, as a nation, Israel is unfaithful, but God is a loving God and faithful to them. This doesn't mean they can continue to sin for they will be judged as will all the unfaithful.

**¹What advantage then has the Jew, or what *is* the profit of circumcision?**

**² Much in every way! Chiefly because to them were committed the [a]oracles of God.**

**³ For what if some did not believe? Will them unbelief makes the faithfulness of God without effect?**

**⁴ Certainly not! Indeed, let God be [b]true but every man a liar. As it is written: "That You may be justified in Your words, And may overcome when You are judged."**

**⁵ But if our unrighteousness demonstrates the righteousness of God, what shall we say? *Is* God unjust who inflicts wrath? (I speak as a man.)**

**⁶ Certainly not! For then how will God judge the world?**

**7 For if the truth of God has increased through my lie to His glory, why am I also still judged as a sinner?**

**8 And *why* not *say,* "Let us do evil that good may come"?—as we are slanderously reported and as some affirm that we say. Their [c]condemnation is just. (Romans 3:1-8 NKJV)**

Paul gets adamant during his next statements. He makes it clear that there is no advantage to being a Jew over the Gentile. All are under sin. The Jews sin with knowledge of the law. Gentile sin with disregard to their God given moral compass. King David tells us 600 years before Paul the state of people in the world.

**1The fool has said in his heart,
"*There is* no God."
They are corrupt,
They have done abominable works,
There is none who does good.**

**2 The LORD looks down from heaven upon the children of men,
To see if there are any who understand, who seek God.**

**3 They have all turned aside,
They have together become corrupt;
*There is* none who does good,
No, not one. (Romans 3:1-3 NKJV)**

There is no difference with the people of the world during Jesus's time and the apostolic period. Paul reminds the Christian Church in Rome that they need to be aware that things have not changed. Jews continue to live by the law and break the law. Pagans continue to worship idols and live by their own individual moralities. Without the "Word" Gentiles have no avenue to salvation. They will be judged according to their works. Then there is the Jew. The law doesn't change the fact that they too are under sin. They will not be justified in God's eyes adhering to the works of the law. Having the law is the conduit for knowledge of sin but provides no hope for salvation.

**⁹ What then? Are we better *than they?* Not at all. For we have previously charged both Jews and Greeks that they are all under sin.**

**¹⁰ As it is written:**

**"There is none righteous, no, not one;**

**¹¹ There is none who understands;
There is none who seeks after God.**

**¹² They have all turned aside;
They have together become unprofitable;
There is none who does good, no, not one."**

**¹³ "Their throat *is* an open [d]tomb;
With their tongues they have practiced deceit";
"The poison of asps *is* under their lips";**

**¹⁴ "Whose mouth *is* full of cursing and bitterness."**

**¹⁵ "Their feet *are* swift to shed blood;**

**¹⁶ Destruction and misery *are* in their ways;**

**¹⁷ And the way of peace they have not known."**

**¹⁸ "There is no fear of God before their eyes."**

**19 Now we know that whatever the law says, it says to those who are under the law, that every mouth may be stopped, and all the world may become [e]guilty before God.**

**20 Therefore by the deeds of the law no flesh will be justified in His sight, for by the law *is* the knowledge of sin. (Romans 3:9-20 NKJV)**

It is clear that there is no salvation under the law. It provides no justification or sanctification in the eyes of God. It is also clear that all people have sinned. In this section is one of the most famous and powerful statements in the Bible.

**23 for all have sinned and fall short of the glory of God, (Romans 3:23 NKJV)**

Through the actions of Adam everybody is subject to the Original Sin. Without distinction everyone is stained with sin and cannot approach the glory of God. In saying "all have sinned" Paul is telling us that we have sinned or will sin. Sin is its own grouping, and all are in it. Whether you are the most moral person or the most heinous person on the planet, you are in the group "Sinner".  This is the criterion that God has established. This is significant because God is just and promises his wrath on anyone who is not sinless. He does not want anyone to compare their sins to his but to compare it to one who was sinless, Jesus. Since God has promised ire and judgement, it is immutable.

Fortunately, Paul provides remediation. Without this, one cannot not be in the presence of God. The remediation to justification is faith in Jesus the Messiah. This of course requires repentance and believing the message of

Jesus. Those who believe in Jesus will obtain salvation as a gift of grace from God.

By faith, we receive this grace. There is no action that one can take to receive this gift. Man is sinful, and until God sent Jesus, man only had the law to try and achieve salvation. This clearly was failing. The sins of man needed to be addressed. The righteous fury of God needs to be satisfied to separate the faithful from the unfaithful. When Jesus was delivered by God to die for our sins on the cross, it was for all man and all sins. This act satisfied God's animus toward sin making God the apologist for all who believe in Jesus.

**21 But now the righteousness of God apart from the law is revealed, being witnessed by the Law and the Prophets,**

**22 even the righteousness of God, through faith in Jesus Christ, to all [f]and on all who believe. For there is no difference;**

**23 for all have sinned and fall short of the glory of God,**

**24 being justified [g]freely by His grace through the redemption that is in Christ Jesus,**

**25 whom God set forth *as* a [h]propitiation by His blood, through faith, to demonstrate His righteousness, because in His forbearance God had passed over the sins that were previously committed,**

**26 to demonstrate at the present time His righteousness, that He might be just and the justifier**

**of the one who has faith in Jesus. (Romans 3:21-26 NKJV)**

Paul ends Chapter III by asking rhetorical questions again. He does this to emphasize the fact that Salvation is a gift of grace available to anyone Jew or Gentile. The law is not a consideration nor are the benevolent activities performed by one. This is not something that can be earned. It is not something that we deserve. It is a free gift that comes by faith.

God's grace gives us repentance and leads us to a changed and improved life. Our hearts become changed. This grace is needed by everyone. Whether it is the atheist or the moralist we all fall "short of the glory of God".

**27 Where *is* boasting then? It is excluded. By what law? Of works? No, but by the law of faith.**

**28 Therefore we conclude that a man is [i]justified by faith apart from the deeds of the law.**

**29 Or *is He* the God of the Jews only? *Is He* not also the God of the Gentiles? Yes, of the Gentiles also, 30 since *there is* one God who will justify the circumcised by faith and the uncircumcised through faith.**

**31 Do we then make void the law through faith? Certainly not! On the contrary, we establish the law. (Romans 3:27-31 NKJV)**

# CHAPTER IV

To clarify faith, Paul uses Abraham the father of the Jewish people as an example. Abraham demonstrated unwavering faith towards God. Whatever was asked of Abraham, he did. When he was told to leave his home in Ur, Mesopotamia (modern day Iraq) and move to Canaan (modern day Syria), he moved. He waited for a son and had Isaac at the age of 99 years old. He was then to sacrifice his beloved son, which he was willing to do because God told him that through him would be a great nation.

Abraham's faith was credited to him as righteousness. God never presented himself in person to Abraham, but Abraham through faith believed in everything God communicated to him. As such, Abraham was justified in the eyes of God. It was not his works that God gave him this gift, it was awarded to him by his faith.

> **¹What then shall we say that Abraham our father[a] has found according to the flesh?**
>
> **² For if Abraham was justified by works, he has *something* to boast about, but not before God.**
>
> **³ For what does the Scripture say? "Abraham believed God, and it was [b]accounted to him for righteousness."**
>
> **⁴ Now to him who works, the wages are not counted [c]as grace but as debt. (Romans 4:1-4 NKJV)**

Paul then speaks of King David. He states that David affirmed the same truths. David speaks of sins that God does not hold one accountable for. They are blessed and given forgiveness by the grace of God.

**5 But to him who does not work but believes on Him who justifies the ungodly, his faith is accounted for righteousness,**

**6 just as David also describes the blessedness of the man to whom God imputes righteousness apart from works:**

**7 "Blessed *is those* whose lawless deeds are forgiven, And whose sins are covered;**

**8 Blessed *is the* man to whom the LORD shall not impute sin." (Romans 4:5-8 NKJV)**

To clear up a common misconception of the time, Paul refers back to Abraham. It was common belief that Abraham was righteous because he was circumcised. Paul makes it clear that this was not the case. Abraham was faithful and considered righteous a long time before he was circumcised. The sequence of events towards righteousness begins with faith. Once faith is established, obedience follows. With unwavering obedience comes righteousness. The seal of righteousness was conferred on Abraham through this process. Years afterwards the Lord told Abraham to accept circumcision as a sign of obedience and a sign of righteousness. To his descendants it became a sign of Israel's faith in God. In Abraham's acceptance of circumcision, he became the spiritual father of all who comes to God through his proxy and son Jesus Christ. This can only happen through faith.

**9 *Does* this blessedness then *come* upon the circumcised *only,* or upon the uncircumcised also? For we say that faith was accounted to Abraham for righteousness.**

**10** How then was it accounted? While he was circumcised, or uncircumcised? Not while circumcised, but while uncircumcised.

**11** And he received the sign of circumcision, a seal of the righteousness of the faith which *he had while still* uncircumcised, that he might be the father of all those who believe, though they are uncircumcised, that righteousness might be imputed to them also,

**12** and the father of circumcision to those who not only *are* of the circumcision, but who also walk in the steps of the faith which our father Abraham *had while still* uncircumcised. (Romans 4:9-12 NKJV)

For those who are righteous through faith, God promises them all they would desire. Yet, this could not be claimed by keeping the law. The law would not be given to the people of Israel for another 430 years when God gave them to Moses. Therefore, it is obvious that law-keeping was not the requirement for the promise of God. Even if law-keeping was the requirement there were none who could continuously keep all 613 Mosaic laws (Drazi,2009).

If law-keeping was the requirement for the promise, what happens to faith. There would be no reason for faith. One would only have to obey the law. Paul clearly details that the law is not sufficient. It is by faith the Abraham's offspring would receive the promises of God.

**13** For the promise that he would be the heir of the world *was* not to Abraham or to his seed through the law, but through the righteousness of faith.

**14** For if those who are of the law *are* heirs, faith is made void and the promise made of no effect,

**15** because the law brings about wrath; for where there is no law *there is* no transgression

**16** Therefore *it is* of faith that *it might be* according to grace, so that the promise might be [d]sure to all the seed, not only to those who are of the law, but also to those who are of the faith of Abraham, who is the father of us all

**17** (as it is written, "I have made you a father of many nations") in the presence of Him whom he believed—God, who gives life to the dead and calls those things which do not exist as though they did;

**18** who, contrary to hope, in hope believed, so that he became the father of many nations, according to what was spoken, "So shall your descendants be."

**19** And not being weak in faith, he did not consider his own body, already dead (since he was about a hundred years old), and the deadness of Sarah's womb. (Romans 4:13-19 NKJV)

Abraham believed anything that God said he would do or say, would come to pass. He had witnessed or experienced this too many times. Paul emphasizes that as Abraham grew older his faith increased. This is why God counted his faith as righteousness. This too is available to all who believe that Jesus paid the price for our sins with his death and that he was resurrected back to life for our justification. By faith any can become justified in the eyes of God.

**20** He did not waver at the promise of God through unbelief, but was strengthened in faith, giving glory to God,

<sup>21</sup> and being fully convinced that what He had promised He was also able to perform.

<sup>22</sup> And therefore "it was accounted to him for righteousness."

<sup>23</sup> Now it was not written for his sake alone that it was imputed to him,

<sup>24</sup> but also for us. It shall be imputed to us who believe in Him who raised up Jesus our Lord from the dead,

<sup>25</sup> who was delivered up because of our offenses, and was raised because of our justification. (Romans 4:20-25 NKJV)

# CHAPTER V

We now understand what it takes to be justified by faith. As Christians we know that we are. Knowing this grants us boundless benefits from God. Since Jesus is our arbitrator to God, he grants us his peace for eternity. Instead of the judgement we deserve for the sins of our past, God provides us grace and good will now that we are redeemed.

**¹Therefore, having been justified by faith, [a]we have peace with God through our Lord Jesus Christ,**

**² through whom also we have access by faith into this grace in which we stand, and rejoice in hope of the glory of God. (Romans 5:1-2 NKJV)**

This does not come easy. There are trials that come with life. There are temptations to overcome. There are sufferings to endure. But those who keep their faith and maintain hope will share in the glories of God.

**³ And not only *that,* but we also glory in tribulations, knowing that tribulation produces [b]perseverance;**

**⁴ and perseverance, [c]character; and character, hope.**

**⁵ Now hope does not disappoint, because the love of God has been poured out in our hearts by the Holy Spirit who was given to us. (Romans 5:3-5 NKJV)**

Paul gives us another truth that is immutable. He wants us to understand that God in his infinite love for us, gave his son for us who are underserving.

**⁸ But God demonstrates His own love toward us, in that while we were still sinners, Christ died for us. (Romans 5:8 NKJV)**

Jesus died for all mankind. If any believes in him, they will be accepted into his family, the family of God. With him we were given the Holy Spirit. We were given the strength of Jesus.

**¹³ I can do all things through [a]Christ who strengthens me. (Philippians 4:13 NKJV)**

God knew that we could not become better on our own. He gave us Jesus to resolve the impediment of sin between himself and man. With Jesus's sacrifice we are no longer enemies of God. Those who believe have been saved unto life eternal. The relationship between God and Christians is one that will last for eternity.

Think about Abraham, he was a man of infinite faith. He was willing to do whatever God asked of him and proved this on multiple occasions. When God asked him to perform the ultimate sacrifice, the sacrifice of his son, he placed all his trust in God and was willing to do as God asked. It was beyond his comprehension what was on God's mind, but he had faith. God takes it a step further; he completes the sacrifice by giving us his son to take away our sins. This is how much he loves us, even while we were still sinners, le loves us.

**⁶ For when we were still without strength, [d]in due time Christ died for the ungodly.**

**7 For scarcely for a righteous man will one die; yet perhaps for a good man someone would even dare to die.**
**8 But God demonstrates His own love toward us, in that while we were still sinners, Christ died for us.**

**9 Much more then, having now been justified by His blood, we shall be saved from wrath through Him.**

**10 For if when we were enemies we were reconciled to God through the death of His Son, much more, having been reconciled, we shall be saved by His life.**

**11 And not only *that,* but we also rejoice in God through our Lord Jesus Christ, through whom we have now received the reconciliation. (Romans 5:6-11 NKJV)**

Paul then gives us his reasoning for our fate. God created Adam and placed him in the Garden of Eden. Adam was without sin. He was given one instruction from God. He was not to eat from the Tree of the Knowledge of Good and Evil.

**17 but of the tree of the knowledge of good and evil you shall not eat, for in the day that you eat of it you[a] shall surely die." (Genesis 2:17 NKJV)**

Adam eventually disobeyed God and introduced sin and death into the world by eating from the Tree of the Knowledge of Good and Evil. This sin was passed down throughout the generations to all man. It was the Catholic bishop Augustine of Hippo who first called this sin the "Original Sin". Through this sin every man is born in sin and shall eventually die.

**12** Therefore, just as through one man sin entered the world, and death through sin, and thus death spread to all men, because all sinned—

**13** (For until the law sin was in the world, but sin is not imputed when there is no law.

**14** Nevertheless death reigned from Adam to Moses, even over those who had not sinned according to the likeness of the transgression of Adam, who is a type of Him who was to come. (Romans 5:12-14 NKJV)

Paul then compares the choice Jesus made to the choice Adam made. Adam's choice led to the sin and death to all man. Jesus was without sin. He never sinned even though he was tempted by all the sins of mankind. Because Jesus never sinned, he brought the chance for all to have life. Jesus was the embodiment of righteousness and through him came the grace of God. Adam's choice brought condemnation; Jesus's choice brought justification.

**15** But the free gift *is* not like the [e]offense. For if by the one man's offense many died, much more the grace of God and the gift by the grace of the one Man, Jesus Christ, abounded to many.

**16** And the gift *is* not like *that which came* through the one who sinned. For the judgment *which came* from one *offense resulted* in condemnation, but the free gift *which came* from many [f]offenses *resulted* in justification.

**17** For if by the one man's [g]offense death reigned through the one, much more those who receive abundance of grace and of the gift of righteousness will reign in life through the One, Jesus Christ.)

**18 Therefore, as through** [h]**one man's offense** *judgment came* **to all men, resulting in condemnation, even so through one**[i] **Man's righteous act** *the free gift came* **to all men, resulting in justification of life.**

**19 For as by one man's disobedience many were made sinners, so also by one Man's obedience many will be made righteous. (Romans 5:15-19 NKJV)**

To end this chapter, Paul offers an interesting twist. He propositions that God's intent for the law was to escalate the amount of lawbreaking on Earth. The law was not intended to make people sin more but to reveal God's Will. With every sin was awareness of wrongdoing. This also reveals the increasing of God's grace to cover the sin. As people believe in Jesus's purpose to sacrifice his life for our sins, God grace increases. That being the case God's grace always covers man's sins.

**20 Moreover the law entered that the offense might abound. But where sin abounded, grace abounded much more,**

**21 so that as sin reigned in death, even so grace might reign through righteousness to eternal life through Jesus Christ our Lord. (Romans 5:20-21 NKJV)**

# CHAPTER VI

The idea of more sin equals more grace is a logical fallacy. Such idea suggesting that more sinning would bring on more grace is contrary to God's will since he does not want us to sin. None can be justified before him if he still harbors sin in his being.

Once a Christian is affirmed to be righteous by God as a result of their faith, they should not continue to sin. Christians are not under the law of Moses which judges and condemns. They are under the grace of God which envelops their sinfulness and removes it as far as East is from the West.

> **¹² As far as the east is from the west,**
> **So far has He removed our transgressions from us.**
> **(Psalms 103:12 NKJV)**

The law pertains to nonbelievers. If righteousness could be attained by the law we would have no need for Jesus. His death would have been in vain. Christians may have the desire to sin on occasion but being in the Spirit makes it easier to resist the temptations. Accepting Christ as our redeemer and savior lets us die a spiritual death to sin and be reborn as a new being with part of Christ within us.

> **²⁰ I have been crucified with Christ; it is no longer I who live, but Christ lives in me; and the *life* which I now live in the flesh I live by faith in the Son of God, who loved me and gave Himself for me. (Galatians 2:20 NKJV)**

Our faith in Jesus has given us a new spiritual life. All Christians go through the same conversion as Jesus did. This is done spiritually. Their old self dies, crucified on the cross. They are buried with him and resurrected to their new life. This new spiritual life has made Jesus a part of every Christian and causes the spiritual death of sin in the process. As Jesus defeated sin in his crucifixion, Christians too have overcome sin and are no longer slave to its temptations. The old self is now dead.

**¹What shall we say then? Shall we continue in sin that grace may abound?**

**² Certainly not! How shall we who died to sin live any longer in it?**

**³ Or do you not know that as many of us as were baptized into Christ Jesus was baptized into His death?**

**⁴ Therefore we were buried with Him through baptism into death, that just as Christ was raised from the dead by the glory of the Father, even so we also should walk in newness of life.**

**⁵ For if we have been united together in the likeness of His death, certainly we also shall be *in the likeness* of *His* resurrection,**

**⁶ knowing this, that our old man was crucified with *Him,* that the body of sin might be [a]done away with, that we should no longer be slaves of sin.**

**⁷ For he who has died has been [b]freed from sin.**

**⁸ Now if we died with Christ, we believe that we shall also live with Him,**

**9** **knowing that Christ, having been raised from the dead, dies no more. Death no longer has dominion over Him.**

**10** **For** *the death* **that He died, He died to sin once for all; but** *the life* **that He lives, He lives to God.**

**11** **Likewise you also,** [c]**reckon yourselves to be dead indeed to sin, but alive to God in Christ Jesus our Lord. (Romans 6:1-11 NKJV)**

At no point is Paul saying that sin is now nonexistence to Christians. He just states that we are no longer under the law where we can be judged and condemned. What he does say is that we can make choices when tempted by sin. And these choices become easier with the help of God.

**13** **No temptation has overtaken you except such as is common to man; but God** *is* **faithful, who will not allow you to be tempted beyond what you are able, but with the temptation will also make the way of escape, that you may be able to** [d]**bear** *it.* **(I Corinthians 10:13 NKJV)**

Even though we are not under the power of sin we will continue to have desire to sin. This is because we are born of sinful nature. Being under God's grace does not remove this. Sinning is natural for man. It takes conscious effort to resist sin and rebuke Satan. So we must not give our bodies over to sin but to give our bodies over to righteousness. We have been resurrected to do God's will.

**12** Therefore do not let sin reign in your mortal body, that you should obey it in its lusts.

**13** And do not present your members *as* [d]instruments of unrighteousness to sin, but present yourselves to God as being alive from the dead, and your members *as* instruments of righteousness to God.

**14** For sin shall not have dominion over you, for you are not under law but under grace. (Romans 6:12-14 NKJV)

This chapter ends with Paul comparing people to either being slaves or free. We are slaves and obedient to sin or slaves and obedient to righteousness. If we chose to be slaves to sin, we know that that will lead to more sin and death. Conversely, if we are slaves to righteousness, we will, by the grace of God, experience eternal life.

**15** What then? Shall we sin because we are not under law but under grace? Certainly not!

**16** Do you not know that to whom you present yourselves slaves to obey, you are that one's slaves whom you obey, whether of sin *leading* to death, or of obedience *leading* to righteousness?

**17** But God be thanked that *though* you were slaves of sin, yet you obeyed from the heart that form of doctrine to which you were [e]delivered.

**18** And having been set free from sin, you became slaves of righteousness.

**19** I speak in human *terms* because of the weakness of your flesh. For just as you presented your members *as* slaves of uncleanness, and of lawlessness *leading* to *more* lawlessness, so now present your members *as* slaves *of* righteousness [f]for holiness.

**20 For when you were slaves of sin, you were free in regard to righteousness.**

**21 What fruits did you have then in the things of which you are now ashamed? For the end of those things *is* death.**

**22 But now having been set free from sin, and having become slaves of God, you have your fruit [g]to holiness, and the end, everlasting life. (Romans 6:15-22 NKJV)**

Paul sums up this discussion with another famous verse from the Bible.

**23 For the wages of sin *is* death, but the [h]gift of God *is* eternal life in Christ Jesus our Lord. (Romans 6:23 NKJV)**

# CHAPTER VII

Paul wants it clear to the Christians of Rome their relationship regarding the law and sin. They must be clear that they are released from the laws of Moses as a result of the surrendering of their lives to Jesus.

He compares the bond of the law to a marriage. A woman whose husband dies frees her from the obligations of marriage and faithfulness to him. She can then marry again without condemnation of adultery. This is similar to one dying to sin and becoming free of the law. One can now enter marriage into Christ and obtain life.

**¹Or do you not know, brethren (for I speak to those who know the law), that the law [a]has dominion over a man as long as he lives?**

**² For the woman who has a husband is bound by the law to *her* husband as long as he lives. But if the husband dies, she is released from the law of *her* husband.**

**³ So then if, while *her* husband lives, she marries another man, she will be called an adulteress; but if her husband dies, she is free from that law, so that she is no adulteress, though she has married another man.**

**⁴ Therefore, my brethren, you also have become dead to the law through the body of Christ, that you may be married to another—to Him who was raised from the dead, that we should bear fruit to God.**

**5** **For when we were in the flesh, the sinful passions which were aroused by the law were at work in our members to bear fruit to death.**

**6** **But now we have been delivered from the law, having died to what we were held by, so that we should serve in the newness of the Spirit and not *in* the oldness of the letter. (Romans 7:1-6 NKJV)**

The bond we have with Jesus is a spiritual death to sin and a resurrection into spiritual life. We now belong to Christ and no man can break this bond. With this bond we can serve God free of the law.

Now Paul wants the Christians to understand that the law is not sinful. He contends that if not for the law his own sins would not have been divulged to him.

**8** **But sin, taking opportunity by the commandment, produced in me all *manner of evil* desire. For apart from the law sin *was* dead. (Romans 7:8 NKJV)**

Once aware of his sins, he felt the need to sin. The law assured him that if he kept the law, he would have life. This was a labor that he could not fulfill. He realized that the law consigned him to death. Nonetheless, the law was necessary and was holy, righteous and virtuous.

**7** **What shall we say then? *Is* the law sin? Certainly not! On the contrary, I would not have known sin except through the law. For I would not have known covetousness unless the law had said, "You shall not covet."**

**8** **But sin, taking opportunity by the commandment, produced in me all *manner of evil* desire. For apart from the law sin *was* dead.**

**9** I was alive once without the law, but when the commandment came, sin revived and I died.

**10** And the commandment, which *was* to *bring* life, I found to *bring* death.

**11** For sin, taking occasion by the commandment, deceived me, and by it killed *me.*

**12** Therefore the law *is* holy, and the commandment holy and just and good. (Romans 7:7-12 NKJV)

Paul tells the Christians that he is not faultless. He too struggles with sin as does anyone whether reborn or not. Even he who is a devout servant of Jesus spiritually is of carnal flesh and subject to imperfection.

**19** For the good that I will *to do,* I do not do; but the evil I will not *to do,* that I practice. (Romans 7:19 NKJV)

Because Paul is born of flesh, he has sinful nature. This is a spiritual attribute that is in all and all struggle with it daily. At times one's behavior surpasses understanding. He is aware that obeying the law can be sinful and this is caused by the evil that is within him.

**13** Has then what is good become death to me? Certainly not! But sin, that it might appear sin, was producing death in me through what is good, so that sin through the commandment might become exceedingly sinful.
**14** For we know that the law is spiritual, but I am carnal, sold under sin.

**15** For what I am doing, I do not understand. For what I will to do, that I do not practice; but what I hate, that I do.

**16** If, then, I do what I will not to do, I agree with the law that *it is* good.

**17** But now, *it is* no longer I who do it, but sin that dwells in me.

**18** For I know that in me (that is, in my flesh) nothing good dwells; for to will is present with me, but *how* to perform what is good I do not find.

**19** For the good that I will *to do,* I do not do; but the evil I will not *to do,* that I practice.

**20** Now if I do what I will not *to do,* it is no longer I who do it, but sin that dwells in me.

**21** I find then a law, that evil is present with me, the one who wills to do good.

**22** For I delight in the law of God according to the inward man.

**23** But I see another law in my members, warring against the law of my mind, and bringing me into captivity to the law of sin which is in my members. (Romans 7:13-23 NKJV

This chapter is speaking to the Judeo-Christian. Being Jewish they were given the law, so Paul is emphatic in his explanation on why they condemned to death through the law. To the Gentile, they did not have the law so they could not be condemned or saved by the law. They were condemned by their lack of belief in Jesus. God gave us Jesus to give salvation to all. Jesus made the law an antiquated means to salvation. That is why the law cannot make one righteous before God. It would be unjust or God to show favoritism on the basis of the law.  Paul's frustration with his own inability to refrain from sin is a metaphor for all man. Christian or not, Jew or Gentile, man is carnal and subordinate to the inherited sinful nature. He cries out to his only hope.

**24 O wretched man that I am! Who will deliver me from this body of death? 25 I thank God—through Jesus Christ our Lord! (Romans 7:24-25 NKJV)**

Only through Jesus is life.

# CHAPTER VIII

Paul tells the Christians of the Roman Church that because of their faith there is no condemnation. This is a promise of God. It can never be changed or broken. His message to all is that having faith in Jesus will deliver the Jewish from the law and the Gentiles from their ignorance of faith. As he has already stated, once one is saved there is nothing that can separate them from God.

Man cannot be saved without faith in Jesus. No matter how much one obeys the law, his flesh is weak and succumbs to sin. Man had lost his way and did not know what the truth was. Thus God sent his son to save man. Through belief in Jesus, sin is defeated, and salvation is attained.

**¹⁶ For God so loved the world that He gave His only begotten Son, that whoever believes in Him should not perish but have everlasting life. (John 3:16 NKJV)**

This is the guarantee from God. If Jesus is rejected, then surely the one who rejects will also be rejected by God. This person lives in the flesh and the flesh is of a carnal mind. Those of a carnal mind cannot please God.

**¹*There is* therefore now no condemnation to those who are in Christ Jesus, who[a] do not walk according to the flesh, but according to the Spirit.**

**² For the law of the Spirit of life in Christ Jesus has made me free from the law of sin and death.**
**³ For what the law could not do in that it was weak through the flesh, God *did* by sending His own Son in**

the likeness of sinful flesh, on account of sin: He condemned sin in the flesh,

**4** that the righteous requirement of the law might be fulfilled in us who do not walk according to the flesh but according to the Spirit.

**5** For those who live according to the flesh set their minds on the things of the flesh, but those *who live* according to the Spirit, the things of the Spirit.

**6** For to be [b]carnally minded *is* death, but to be spiritually minded *is* life and peace.

**7** Because the [c]carnal mind *is* enmity against God; for it is not subject to the law of God, nor indeed can be.

**8** So then, those who are in the flesh cannot please God. (Romans 8:1-8 NKJV)

Every Christian has the Holy Spirit in them. This was given to them at the crucifixion of Christ.

**20** I have been crucified with Christ; it is no longer I who live, but Christ lives in me; and the *life* which I now live in the flesh I live by faith in the Son of God, who loved me and gave Himself for me. (Galatians 2:20 NKJV)

This same Holy Spirit resurrects us to life as it did in Jesus. This life in the flesh is powered by the Holy Spirit. The deeper meaning of this verse is that of life and death. Life through righteousness of the Holy Spirit and conversely death to sin through the Holy Spirit.

**9** But you are not in the flesh but in the Spirit, if indeed the Spirit of God dwells in you. Now if anyone does not have the Spirit of Christ, he is not His.

**10** And if Christ *is* in you, the body *is* dead because of sin, but the Spirit *is* life because of righteousness.

**11** But if the Spirit of Him who raised Jesus from the dead dwells in you, He who raised Christ from the dead will also give life to your mortal bodies [d]through His Spirit who dwells in you. (Romans 8:9-11 NKJV)

The Spirit of God dwells in us. This allows us to be adopted into the family of God. It also makes us indebted to God. Not to fear him as slaves to him, but to be reverent to him as sons and daughters. We share this kinship with Jesus for all eternity.

**12** Therefore, brethren, we are debtors—not to the flesh, to live according to the flesh.

**13** For if you live according to the flesh you will die; but if by the Spirit you put to death the deeds of the body, you will live.

**14** For as many as are led by the Spirit of God, these are sons of God.

**15** For you did not receive the spirit of bondage again to fear, but you received the Spirit of adoption by whom we cry out, "Abba,[e] Father."

**16** The Spirit Himself bears witness with our spirit that we are children of God,

**17 and if children, then heirs—heirs of God and joint heirs with Christ, if indeed we suffer with *Him,* that we may also be glorified together. (Romans 8:12-17 NKJV)**

But we also share in Jesus's anguish. Though Jesus is finished with his suffering and is In heaven sitting at the right hand of God, we suffer on a daily basis in this corrupt world.  However, this suffering is in no comparison to the splendors of heaven.

As it is inevitable to suffer, Paul explains this is associated with pain. This pain is shared with all creation as we wait for the revealing of God's children. When this occurs the children of God will complete their adoption into the into their new redemptive bodies that will be acceptable to God. This is what we hope for. This is our faith in the sacrifice of Jesus for our salvation.

**18 For I consider that the sufferings of this present time are not worthy *to be compared* with the glory which shall be revealed in us.**

**19 For the earnest expectation of the creation eagerly waits for the revealing of the sons of God.**

**20 For the creation was subjected to futility, not willingly, but because of Him who subjected *it* in hope;**

**21 because the creation itself also will be delivered from the bondage of [f]corruption into the glorious liberty of the children of God.**

**22 For we know that the whole creation groans and labors with birth pangs together until now.**

**23** Not only *that,* but we also who have the first fruits of the Spirit, even we ourselves groan within ourselves, eagerly waiting for the adoption, the redemption of our body.

**24** For we were saved in this hope, but hope that is seen is not hope; for why does one still hope for what he sees?

**25** But if we hope for what we do not see, we eagerly wait for *it* with perseverance. (Romans 8:18-25 NKJV)

God knows we are suffering and in pain for our sufferings. In these times of trouble, we pray. We pray for God's help. Sometimes we are in so much pain we don't know how to ask for help. The Lord knows our heart and does not want us to feel abandoned. So when we are reborn, God becomes part of us in the form of the Holy Spirit. The Holy Spirit will make intercession for us when we are in these desperate situations.

**26** Likewise the Spirit also helps in our weaknesses. For we do not know what we should pray for as we ought, but the Spirit Himself makes intercession [g]for us with groanings which cannot be uttered.

**27** Now He who searches the hearts knows what the mind of the Spirit *is,* because He makes intercession for the saints according to *the will of* God. (Romans 8:26-27 NKJV)

God would not leave us without help because he chose us before we were even born. We are part of God's ultimate plan. We were chosen for his purpose to imitate his son and whoever he chose was destined to be justified in his eyes. One thing that we could believe in without a doubt is that with God on our side all things will turn out for the good.

**28 And we know that all things work together for good to those who love God, to those who are the called according to *His* purpose.**

**29 For whom He foreknew, He also predestined *to be* conformed to the image of His Son, that He might be the firstborn among many brethren.**

**30 Moreover whom He predestined, these He also called; whom He called, these He also justified; and whom He justified, these He also glorified. (Romans 8:28-30 NKJV)**

Verse 28 needs to be repeated because it is very important for our understanding of our destiny and what God thought of us. We who love God are part of a plan that only he knows the beginning and the end. We need to trust in his will and have trust in his purpose for us. God will direct our path.

**28 And we know that all things work together for good to those who love God, to those who are the called according to *His* purpose.**

God is our protector and provider. Every Christian that has ever existed and who will exist was chosen by God before they ever knew him. He stands for us no matter who is in opposition to us. He is omnipotent, omnipresent and omniscient. Paul asks the rhetorical question,

**31 What then shall we say to these things? If God *is* for us, who *can be* against us? (Romans 8:31 NKJV)**

We must have faith in God's everlasting love for us. He gave us his son to take away all our sins past, present and future. Jesus gave his blood and his life for us on the cross that we may be justified in the eyes of his father. He rose from the dead that we too may be of the firstborn to not die but live for eternity with him in heaven. So, whatever the situation is, no matter how abysmal life may seem, there is nothing in creation that can separate us from God's love for us through Jesus Christ.

**31 What then shall we say to these things? If God *is* for us, who *can be* against us?**

**32 He who did not spare His own Son, but delivered Him up for us all, how shall He not with Him also freely give us all things?**

**33 Who shall bring a charge against God's elect? *It is* God who justifies.**

**34 Who *is* he who condemns? *It is* Christ who died, and furthermore is also risen, who is even at the right hand of God, who also makes intercession for us.**

**35 Who shall separate us from the love of Christ? *Shall* tribulation, or distress, or persecution, or famine, or nakedness, or peril, or sword?**

**36 As it is written:**
> **"For Your sake we are killed all day long;**
> **We are accounted as sheep for the slaughter."**

**37 Yet in all these things we are more than conquerors through Him who loved us.**

**38** For I am persuaded that neither death nor life, nor angels nor principalities nor powers, nor things present nor things to come,

**39** nor height nor depth, nor any other created thing, shall be able to separate us from the love of God which is in Christ Jesus our Lord. Romans 8:31-39 NKJV)

# CHAPTER IX

Paul is distraught about the state of the people of Israel. He was born into both the world of the Jewish and the world of the Romans. Paul was Hebrew by nationality who was born in the province of Cilicia. This was in the city of Tarsus which was a "free city" of Rome (Dunn,2003). Though he was Jewish, being born in Tarsus granted him Roman citizenship. Paul was raised in the Jewish religion and traditions. Like his father, he was a Pharisee.

Paul was distraught because the people of Israel had rejected Jesus. Few accepted the message of Christ, but the majority, bound by tradition and the law would not believe in Jesus being the Messiah. Paul went through great effort to convince first the Jews then the Gentiles that the law would not save them from the wrath of God. In his despair, Paul declares that he would rather be separated from Jesus if only his people would come to Him. Paul could not understand how the people of Israel reject Jesus since God had given them such privilege as his chosen people.

He list these gifts that God gave only to the Jewish people, the most important being the bequeathing of his son. Above all, God will always keep his promises.

> **1 I tell the truth in Christ, I am not lying, my conscience also bearing me witness in the Holy Spirit,**
>
> **2 that I have great sorrow and continual grief in my heart.**
>
> **3 For I could wish that I myself were accursed from Christ for my brethren, my [a]countrymen according to the flesh,**

**⁴ who are Israelites, to whom *pertain* the adoption, the glory, the covenants, the giving of the law, the service *of God,* and the promises;**

**⁵ of whom *are* the fathers and from whom, according to the flesh, Christ *came,* who is over all, *the* eternally blessed God. Amen. (Romans 9:1-5 NKJV)**

Paul makes a distinction between the children of God and everyone else. Just because one is born of Israel this doesn't make them automatically a child of God. Those who are children of the flesh are not Israelites, not of the seed of Abraham. These children of the flesh may have been born Jewish, but they surely will not evade God's wrath.

**⁶ But it is not that the word of God has taken no effect. For they *are* not all Israel who *are* of Israel,**

**⁷ nor *are they* all children because they are the seed of Abraham; but, "In Isaac your seed shall be called."**

**⁸ That is, those who *are* the children of the flesh, these *are* not the children of God; but the children of the promise are counted as the seed. (Romans 9:6-8 NKJV)**

God gives mercy to whomever he chooses. Paul refers to the Old Testament to make this point clear. God made his covenant with Abraham because of his faith. He blessed his wife Sarah with a son, Isaac, at the age of 90 years old.  Through Isaac would come all the children of Israel. Isaac, through his wife Rebecca gave us the twins Esau and Jacob. Before they were born, God told Rebecca that the younger would rule over the older. Then he speaks of Moses who God said that he would give mercy and compassion to whomever he chooses. God overwhelmed the Egyptian Pharaoh Neferhotep l with 10 plagues in order to increase his own glory.  The point is that not all are children of Israel and to those God does not have a covenant. It is up to his discretion who he will show mercy.

**9 For this *is* the word of promise: "At this time I will come and Sarah shall have a son."**

**10 And not only *this*, but when Rebecca also had conceived by one man, *even* by our father Isaac**

**11 (for *the children* not yet being born, nor having done any good or evil, that the purpose of God according to election might stand, not of works but of Him who calls),**

**12 it was said to her, "The older shall serve the younger."**

**13 As it is written, "Jacob I have loved, but Esau I have hated."**

**14 What shall we say then? *Is there* unrighteousness with God? Certainly not!**

**15 For He says to Moses, "I will have mercy on whomever I will have mercy, and I will have compassion on whomever I will have compassion."**

**16 So then *it is* not of him who wills, nor of him who runs, but of God who shows mercy.**

**17 For the Scripture says to the Pharaoh, "For this very purpose I have raised you up, that I may show My power in you, and that My name may be declared in all the earth."**

**18 Therefore He has mercy on whom He wills, and whom He wills He hardens. (Romans 9:6-18 NKJV)**

Paul answers questions that he suspects the people will ask. He challenges them by asking them who would question the motives of God. His presents an analogy of God being the potter and humans being the clay. He could fashion the clay in forms for good or forms for sin, vessels if you will.

But what if God had long term plans for the vessel forms for sin. If the long-term plans would ultimately reveal his glory what would mortals know of this. How would they know that God would tolerate the dishonorable vessels to ultimately show his mercy.

**19 You will say to me then, "Why does He still find fault? For who has resisted His will?"**

**20 But indeed, O man, who are you to reply against God? Will the thing formed say to him who formed *it*, "Why have you made me like this?"**

**21 Does not the potter have power over the clay, from the same lump to make one vessel for honor and another for dishonor?**

**22 *What* if God, wanting to show *His* wrath and to make His power known, endured with much longsuffering the vessels of wrath prepared for destruction,**

**23 and that He might make known the riches of His glory on the vessels of mercy, which He had prepared beforehand for glory,**

**24 even us whom He called, not of the Jews only, but also of the Gentiles? (Romans 9:19-24 NKJV)**

Over 700 hundred years earlier Hosea and Isaiah prophesized what would become of the Gentiles and Jewish people. Paul quotes from Hosea that there will be Gentiles called to become God's people. He quotes from Isaiah the calling of a remnant of natural born Israelites to become God's people. The people he calls, Gentiles or Jewish, are called through faith in Jesus Christ. It is unfortunate for the Jews who stumble because they put their faith in the law, not the Divine Law but the whole of the Mosaic laws.

**25 As He says also in Hosea:**

> **"I will call them My people, who were not My people,**
> **And her beloved, who was not beloved."**

> **26 "And it shall come to pass in the place where it was said to them,**
> **'You *are* not My people,'**
> **There they shall be called sons of the living God."**

**27 Isaiah also cries out concerning Israel:**

> **"Though the number of the children of Israel be as the sand of the sea,**
> **The remnant will be saved.**

> **28 For [b]He will finish the work and cut *it* short in righteousness,**
> **Because the LORD will make a short work upon the earth."**

**29 And as Isaiah said before:**

"Unless the LORD of [c]Sabaoth had left us a seed,
We would have become like Sodom,
And we would have been made like Gomorrah."

30 What shall we say then? That Gentiles, who did not pursue righteousness, have attained to righteousness, even the righteousness of faith;

31 but Israel, pursuing the law of righteousness, has not attained to the law [d]of righteousness.

32 Why? Because *they did* not *seek it* by faith, but as it were, [e]by the works of the law. For they stumbled at that stumbling stone.

33 As it is written:

"Behold, I lay in Zion a stumbling stone and rock of offense,

And whoever believes on Him will not be put to shame." (Romans 9:25-33 NKJV)

# CHAPTER X

Paul being the Jews Jew has a heavy heart because his people did not grasp the significance of rejecting Jesus. Israel's path to righteousness was mistaken and Paul was fervently trying to make them understand the error of their way. The law could not save anyone. The prophets of ancient times spoke of this throughout the Old Testament. The people of Israel refused to come to God through faith in Jesus Christ.

Paul prays for Israel to be redeemed. He knows that they honestly believe in God and believe that the law will redeem them. For the majority, they refused to even hear the message of Jesus. They did not understand that Jesus was the end of the law and righteousness to everyone who believes.

> **[1]Brethren, my heart's desire and prayer to God for [a]Israel is that they may be saved.**
>
> **[2] For I bear them witness that they have a zeal for God, but not according to knowledge.**
>
> **[3] For they being ignorant of God's righteousness, and seeking to establish their own righteousness, have not submitted to the righteousness of God.**
>
> **[4] For Christ is the end of the law for righteousness to everyone who believes. (Romans 10:1-4 NKJV**

Moses gave the children of Israel the law. He explained how living by the law will attain righteousness. But Moses was wrong. Those who live by the law will not be redeemed. The Jewish people continue to live by the law, and they continue to break the law. They continue to speculate on whether they will spend eternity with God or whether they would spend eternity in Hell. We know that Jesus had been in both places. He was in heaven in the beginning, he died, descended into Hell then rose and ascended to Heaven to sit at the right hand of God. So we know that redemption comes through faith in the one who was the firstborn resurrected. This grace is not to favor the Jew over the Gentile but is given to anyone who has faith.

> **5 For Moses writes about the righteousness which is of the law, "The man who does those things shall live by them."**
>
> **6 But the righteousness of faith speaks in this way, "Do not say in your heart, 'Who will ascend into heaven?'" (that is, to bring Christ down *from above*)**
>
> **7 or, "'Who will descend into the abyss?'" (that is, to bring Christ up from the dead).**
>
> **8 But what does it say? "The word is near you, in your mouth and in your heart" (that is, the word of faith which we preach): (Romans 10:5-8 NKJV)**

Paul then makes one of the most profound statements in the Bible.

> **9 that if you confess with your mouth the Lord Jesus and believe in your heart that God has raised Him from the dead, you will be saved.**
>
> **10 For with the heart one believes unto righteousness, and with the mouth confession is made unto salvation. (Romans 10:9-10 NKJV)**

In this statement, Paul makes it clear how one has an opportunity to be saved. This is only done through faith in Jesus and this salvation is available to everyone. No matter what belief someone has, they have an opportunity to be saved.

**11 For the Scripture says, "Whoever believes on Him will not be put to shame."**

**12 For there is no distinction between Jew and Greek, for the same Lord over all is rich to all who call upon Him.**

**13 For "whoever calls on the name of the LORD shall be saved." (Romans 10:11-13 NKJV)**

This is why Paul preaches. He was commissioned to save first the Jews and then the Gentiles. Paul knows the message of Jesus. He knows that to be saved they must come to know and believe in Jesus. In order for this to happen they must hear. This is why Paul must preach the word of God.

**17 So then faith *comes* by hearing, and hearing by the word of God. (Romans 10:17 NKJV)**

Still, many will listen but will not hear. This is especially true for the Jewish people. And even though many Gentiles listen to the truth of the gospel of Jesus they too will continue to refuse to hear. Those who refuse to hear will oppose Paul, but he must preach nonetheless.

**14 How then shall they call on Him in whom they have not believed? And how shall they believe in Him of whom they have not heard? And how shall they hear without a preacher?**

**15 And how shall they preach unless they are sent? As it is written:**

> "How beautiful are the feet of those
> who [b]preach the gospel of peace,
> Who bring glad tidings of good things!"

**16** But they have not all obeyed the gospel. For Isaiah says, "LORD, who has believed our report?"

**17** So then faith *comes* by hearing, and hearing by the word of God.

**18** But I say, have they not heard? Yes indeed:
> "Their sound has gone out to all the earth,
> And their words to the ends of the world."
> (Romans 10:14-18 NKJV)

Knowing that the people of Israel has heard the gospel, could they not understand? Could they not comprehend that salvation comes by faith in Jesus. God through Moses told the Jewish people that nations would be jealous because of the Word given to them. He then quotes Isaiah who prophesizes about those who were not called, Gentiles, who will believe in Jesus. Yet, God is patient and will wait for the Jewish people to come back to him. If they should return to him.

**19** But I say, did Israel not know? First Moses says:
> "I will provoke you to jealousy by *those who are* not a nation,
> I will move you to anger by a foolish nation."

**20** But Isaiah is very bold and says:
> "I was found by those who did not seek Me;
> I was made manifest to those who did not ask for Me."

**21** But to Israel he says:

"All day long I have stretched out My hands
To a disobedient and contrary people." (Romans
10:19-21 NKJV)

# CHAPTER XI

In Chapters 9 and 10 Paul is speaking mostly of the Jews. He speaks of how the reject Jesus and why they need Jesus. He discusses the law and how salvation does not come from the law. Questioning rhetorically again, he ask will God cast away the people of Israel? Emphatically he says no. God has chosen these people. He has nurtured them since he made a covenant with Abraham to be their God. We know though there is rejection of Jesus Christ with the people of Israel, God patiently waits for them.

**⁸The Lᴏʀᴅ *is* merciful and gracious, Slow to anger, and abounding in mercy. (Psalms 103:8 NKJV)**

Paul knows that he is saved by his faith in Jesus, and he surely is a Jew. A Jews Jew who not only passionately believed in God but enthusiastically embraced and practiced Jewish law as a Pharisee. This all changed when he came to have faith in Jesus and the message of salvation. If he, the greatest antagonist of Jesus could be saved, then salvation is possible for all Jewish person. He knows that this will not be possible for the majority of the Jews but for those who do accept Jesus he calls the "remnant" as did the prophet Elijah.

**¹I say then, has God cast away His people? Certainly not! For I also am an Israelite, of the seed of Abraham, *of* the tribe of Benjamin.**

**² God has not cast away His people whom He foreknew. Or do you not know what the Scripture says of Elijah, how he pleads with God against Israel, saying,**

**3** "LORD, they have killed Your prophets and torn down Your altars, and I alone am left, and they seek my life"?

**4** But what does the divine response say to him? "I have reserved for Myself seven thousand men who have not bowed the knee to Baal."

**5** Even so then, at this present time there is a remnant according to the election of grace. (Romans 11:1-5 NKJV)

With the law the people of Israel must prove their worth for salvation through works. They do not understand that this is not necessary. Paul wants them to understand that if works will provide them a path to salvation, then there is no need for grace.

**6** And if by grace, then *it is* no longer of works; otherwise, grace is no longer grace. [a]but if *it is* of works, it is no longer grace; otherwise, work is no longer work. (Romans 11:6 NKJV)

In our modern times do we understand this concept? God's grace is one of the most fundamental doctrines of Christianity. Without God's grace, Christianity does not even exist. Grace as defined by Merriam-Webster as,

**a:** unmerited divine assistance given to humans for their regeneration or sanctification

**b:** a virtue coming from God

**c:** a state of sanctification enjoyed through divine assistance

Grace is unmerited. Grace is given to us by God. We do not deserve it. We do not earn it. No matter how many good works we perform, grace would not be part of that conversation.

> **8 For by grace you have been saved through faith, and that not of yourselves; *it is* the gift of God, 9 not of works, lest anyone should boast. (Ephesians 2:8-9 NKJV)**

Is it not foretold though, that the children of Israel would have hardened hearts? God would blind them and deafen their ears to the gospel of Jesus. Approximately 1,500 years earlier Moses made the prophetic statement,

> **3 the great trials which your eyes have seen, the signs, and those great wonders.**

> **4 Yet the LORD has not given you a heart to [a]perceive and eyes to see and ears to hear, to this *very* day. (Deuteronomy 29:3-4 NKJV)**

Paul then references King David's assessment of the plight of the children of Isarel 700 years earlier. He refers to the message as a stumbling block to their darkened eyes.

> **7 What then? Israel has not obtained what it seeks; but the elect has obtained it, and the rest were blinded.**

> **8 Just as it is written:**
> **"God has given them a spirit of stupor,**
> **Eyes that they should not see**
> **And ears that they should not hear,**
> **To this very day."**

**⁹ And David says:**
**"Let their table become a snare and a trap,**
**A stumbling block and a recompense to them.**

**¹⁰ Let their eyes be darkened, so that they do not see,**
**And bow down their back always." (Romans 11:7-10**
**NKJV)**

Paul surmises that a reason for Jewish unbelief is to allow inclusivity of Gentiles into Jesus's family. He likens Jesus to being a tree and the Gentiles who come to believe in Jesus as being the new branches grafted onto that tree. The old branches that are unbelieving Jews have broken away to allow for these new branches. His hope is that this would provoke the Jewish to jealously about the Gentiles standing in the eyes of God. The Jewish know Paul is one of their own and see him proselytize to the Gentiles. In this way some might be drawn to Jesus and be saved.

**¹¹ I say then, have they stumbled that they should fall? Certainly not! But through their [b]fall, to provoke them to jealousy, salvation *has come* to the Gentiles.**

**¹² Now if their [c]fall *is* riches for the world, and their failure riches for the Gentiles, how much more their fullness!**

**¹³ For I speak to you Gentiles; inasmuch as I am an apostle to the Gentiles, I magnify my ministry, ¹⁴ if by any means I may provoke to jealousy *those who are* my flesh and save some of them.**

**¹⁵ For if their being cast away *is* the reconciling of the world, what *will* their acceptance *be* but life from the dead?**

**16 For if the first fruit *is* holy, the lump *is* also *holy;* and if the root *is* holy, so *are* the branches. (Romans 11:11-16 NKJV)**

Paul then tells the Gentile believers to not be condescending or arrogant. They must remember that God chose them and made the tree to support them. They were not chosen to be the support for the tree. He reminds the Gentile believers that if God would cut off his own people, the same could happen to them. Even the believer must be ever vigilant to the evils of the world and obedient to the Lord lest they be cut off too.

Though the branches have fallen off, God is not finished with them. There will come a time when allotted number of Gentiles will be complete. At this time God will soften the hearts of his people and they will realize the truth. The Jewish people will listen and now hear. They will then turn to Jesus and then will be grafted back onto the tree.

**17 And if some of the branches were broken off, and you, being a wild olive tree, were grafted in among them, and with them became a partaker of the root and [d]fatness of the olive tree,**

**18 do not boast against the branches. But if you do boast, *remember that* you do not support the root, but the root *supports* you.**

**19 You will say then, "Branches were broken off that I might be grafted in."**

**20 Well *said.* Because of unbelief they were broken off, and you stand by faith. Do not be haughty, but fear.**

**21 For if God did not spare the natural branches, He may not spare you either.**

**22 Therefore consider the goodness and severity of God: on those who fell, severity; but toward you, [e]goodness, if you continue in *His* goodness. Otherwise, you also will be cut off.**

**23 And they also, if they do not continue in unbelief, will be grafted in, for God is able to graft them in again.**

**24 For if you were cut out of the olive tree which is wild by nature, and were grafted contrary to nature into a cultivated olive tree, how much more will these, who *are* natural *branches,* be grafted into their own olive tree? (Romans 11:17-24 NKJV)**

The children of Israel are in an awkward position with the gospel. As a group they love God and God loves them. He has since the covenant was made with them when they became a people. Spiritually they hate what Paul is preaching. They cannot be followers of Jesus because they are blinded and deafened by God. This makes them enemies of the gospel of Jesus and have become disconnected from salvation lack of faith. They are stuck on the Mosaic laws which require works instead of faith.

God uses his mercy and grace given to the Gentiles to make the Jewish people jealous. The purpose is to have his people come back to him.as a nation. It will take time for that to happen but over time individual Jews will accept the gospel and trust in Jesus. What we know from this is that Israel's rejection of Jesus is not total or final.

**25 For I do not desire, brethren, that you should be ignorant of this mystery, lest you should be wise in your own [f]opinion, that blindness in part has**

happened to Israel until the fullness of the Gentiles has come in.

**26** And so all Israel will be [g]saved, as it is written:

> "The Deliverer will come out of Zion,
> And He will turn away ungodliness from Jacob;
> **27** For this *is* My covenant with them,
> When I take away their sins."

**28** Concerning the gospel *they are* enemies for your sake, but concerning the election *they are* beloved for the sake of the fathers.

**29** For the gifts and the calling of God *are* irrevocable. **30** For as you were once disobedient to God, yet have now obtained mercy through their disobedience,

**31** even so these also have now been disobedient, that through the mercy shown you they also may obtain mercy.

**32** For God has [h]committed them all to disobedience, that He might have mercy on all. (Romans 11:25-32 NKJV)

In the end, who can know the depth of God's wisdom and knowledge. We cannot know his mind or where his benevolence is directed. For everything is for him and through him and the glory belongs to him.

**33** Oh, the depth of the riches both of the wisdom and knowledge of God! How unsearchable *are* His judgments and His ways past finding out!

[34] "For who has known the mind of the LORD?
Or who has become His counselor?"

[35] "Or who has first given to Him
And it shall be repaid to him?"

[36] For of Him and through Him and to Him *are* all things, to whom *be* glory forever. Amen. (Romans 11:33-36 NKJV)

# CHAPTER XII

Paul begins a new segment of his letter. In the first 11 chapters of his letter, he teaches the doctrine of salvation and how to live according to the truths thereof. The truth being, we are saved by the grace of God and this grace is given by one's faith in Jesus Christ his son.

> **¹I beseech[a] you therefore, brethren, by the mercies of God, that you present your bodies a living sacrifice, holy, acceptable to God, *which is* your [b]reasonable service. (Romans 12:1 NKJV)**

So how does one give homage to the mercy and grace of God. They do this by worship. Not period worship, but giving of one's whole being, our entire life to God. We are to become living sacrifices giving what life God has given to us for his glory. Paul tells us that we are to give up the way of the world and be transformed with the renewing of our mind to see the world through the eyes of God. In this way we begin to understand God's will.

> **² And do not be conformed to this world, but be transformed by the renewing of your mind, that you may prove what *is* that good and acceptable and perfect will of God. (Romans 12:-2 NKJV)**

Paul tells us that we are all members of the one body. Jesus is the head, and we are members comprising the body. When we were saved, as part of his grace, God gave us the Holy Spirit. Through the Holy Spirit we are each given spiritual gifts that we can serve each other and also our fellow man. Correspondingly, as members of Christ body we all do not have the same spiritual gifts. There is differentiation assigned by the Holy Spirit.  This is what keeps the body flourishing, all members performing their given spiritual gifts.

> **³ For I say, through the grace given to me, to everyone who is among you, not to think *of himself* more highly than he ought to think, but to think soberly, as God has dealt to each one a measure of faith.**
>
> **⁴ For as we have many members in one body, but all the members do not have the same function,**
>
> **⁵ so we, *being* many, are one body in Christ, and individually members of one another.**
>
> **⁶ Having then gifts differing according to the grace that is given to us, *let us use them:* if prophecy, *let us prophesy* in proportion to our faith;**
>
> **⁷ or ministry, *let us use it* in *our* ministering; he who teaches, in teaching;**
>
> **⁸ he who exhorts, in exhortation; he who gives, with liberality; he who leads, with diligence; he who shows mercy, with cheerfulness. (Romans 12:3-8 NKJV)**

We then must live the Christian life with Jesus as our role model. This life does not occur overnight but becomes more apparent as we increase our relationship with God through faith in his son Jesus Christ. First and foremost, we must rebuke Satan and all the evil he represents. We must seek good always. Never should we forsake the divine laws of God. These are the 10 Commandments that are paraphrased by Jesus.

**37** Jesus said to him, "'You shall love the LORD your God with all your heart, with all your soul, and with all your mind.'

**38** This is *the* first and great commandment.

**39** And *the* second *is* like it: 'You shall love your neighbor as yourself.'

**40** On these two commandments hang all the Law and the Prophets." (Matthew 22:37-40 NKJV)

Living by these divine laws requires one love without hypocrisy. Always serve the Lord by staying in the spirit. Our actions should be genuine, never forced but completed in love.

**9** *Let* love *be* without hypocrisy. Abhor what is evil. Cling to what is good.

**10** *Be* kindly affectionate to one another with brotherly love, in honor giving preference to one another;

**11** not lagging in diligence, fervent in spirit, serving the Lord;

**12** rejoicing in hope, patient[c] in tribulation, continuing steadfastly in prayer;

**13** distributing to the needs of the saints, given[d] to hospitality. (Romans 12:9-13 NKJV)

Life is short and we must live it for God. We have been saved by the grace of God and should be eternally happy for this blessing. We must never give into the ways of the world but must keep humble and seek the Lord for wisdom.

We also must remember to love our enemies. It is easy to love our friends and family but to love one's enemies requires help from the Lord. This requires us to forgive. Yes, life will be challenging and at times the trials may be difficult, but we cannot assign blame to people for their actions against us. Jesus tells us to not take vengeance. Live among your enemy as best as you can as evil should never be repaid with like action. It is not our place to judge. We place our hope in God, it is his place to take vengeance.

**14 Bless those who persecute you; bless and do not curse.**

**15 Rejoice with those who rejoice, and weep with those who weep.**

**16 Be of the same mind toward one another. Do not set your mind on high things, but associate with the humble. Do not be wise in your own opinion.**

**17 Repay no one evil for evil. Have[e] regard for good things in the sight of all men.**

**18 If it is possible, as much as depends on you, live peaceably with all men.**

**19 Beloved, do not avenge yourselves, but *rather* give place to wrath; for it is written, "Vengeance *is* Mine, I will repay," says the Lord.**

**20 Therefore**

**"If your enemy is hungry, feed him;
If he is thirsty, give him a drink;
For in so doing you will hear coals of fire on his
head."**

**21 Do not be overcome by evil, but overcome evil with
good. (Romans 12:14-21 NKJV)**

Let our mind always be committed to the life of sacrifice. Commit our mind, body, heart, and soul daily and live by the divine laws.

# CHAPTER XIII

Paul reminds the Christian Church to be subject to the governing bodies of the earth. These authorities are not placed there on their own accord, but by God for his purpose. This is all part of the plan he has in store for man. Therefore, obeying the authorities is obeying God, while on the other hand, disobeying the authorities is in opposition to God's will.

> **¹ Let every soul be subject to the governing authorities. For there is no authority except from God, and the authorities that exist are appointed by God.**
>
> **² Therefore whoever resists the authority resists the ordinance of God, and those who resist will [a]bring judgment on themselves. (Romans 13:1-2 NKJV)**

God has placed governments in place to do his will. People have inherited sinful nature from Adam and throughout history and do bad things. Governments are in place to uphold a social contract with the people to protect those who do good things from those who do bad things among other things. For those who do good things, there is nothing to fear. Conversely, those who do bad things will bring the judgement of governments down upon them. They live in fear as they know they are wrong and are being disobedient to the law. Therefore, any judgement from the government is by proxy from God.

> **³ For rulers are not a terror to good works, but to evil. Do you want to be unafraid of the authority? Do what is good, and you will have praise from the same.**

**4 For he is God's minister to you for good. But if you do evil, be afraid; for he does not bear the sword in vain; for he is God's minister, an avenger to *execute* wrath on him who practices evil. (Romans 2:3-4 NKJV)**

Through the course of our daily lives, we must strive to do good. Not out of fear from the judgement and punishment from the authorities but from consciousness of our moral barometer. So to the governments, we must respect and obey them since this system was set up by God. Thus, we are obligated to pay their taxes to support God's given authority.

**5 Therefore *you* must be subject, not only because of wrath but also for conscience' sake.**

**6 For because of this you also pay taxes, for they are God's ministers attending continually to this very thing.**

**7 Render therefore to all their due: taxes to whom taxes *are due,* customs to whom customs, fear to whom fear, honor to whom honor. (Romans 13:5-7 NKJV)**

Jesus told us to love one another as we would ourselves.

**39 And *the* second *is* like it: 'You shall love your neighbor as yourself.' (Matthew 22:39 NKJV)**

Paul wanted to make sure that it was understood that this was a summary of the last six divine commandments. If we follow this summarization of the commandments, then we will have fulfilled the law. Love causes no harm.

**¹³ And now abide faith, hope, love, these three; but the greatest of these *is* love. (I Corinthians 13:13 NKJV)**

Jesus lived his life according to this premise. No matter how persecuted he was, no matter how tortured he was, even to his death, he loved man. This type of love he taught all his disciples and commissioned then to therefore teach all of their disciples.

**⁸ Owe no one anything except to love one another, for he who loves another has fulfilled the law.**

**⁹ For the commandments, "You shall not commit adultery," "You shall not murder," "You shall not steal," [b] "You shall not bear false witness," "You shall not covet," and if *there is* any other commandment, are *all* summed up in this saying, namely, "You shall love your neighbor as yourself."**

**¹⁰ Love does no harm to a neighbor; therefore, love *is* the fulfil**

Paul speaks to the church about the return of Jesus. He reminds them that there will be a judgement. He uses the metaphor of the night ending and the day coming to represent that time is short and all believers must be prepared. Christians must resist evil and do good. Christian life should be dedicated to living as Jesus did. As Paul had stated earlier, imitate his lifestyle and abandon all things related to worldly sinful nature. Paul states that we must put on the "armor of light" as darkness cannot prevail in the light.

**11** And *do* this, knowing the time, that now *it is* high time to awake out of sleep; for now, our salvation *is* nearer than when we *first* believed.

**12** The night is far spent; the day is at hand. Therefore, let us cast off the works of darkness, and let us put on the armor of light.

**13** Let us walk [c]properly, as in the day, not in revelry and drunkenness, not in lewdness and lust, not in strife and envy.

**14** But put on the Lord Jesus Christ, and make no provision for the flesh, to *fulfill its* lusts. (Romans 13:11-14 NKJV)

# CHAPTER XIV

Paul acknowledges that there are two types of Christians in the Roman Church. There are those who completely believe without doubt in their faith, then there are those who are weaker in faith and aren't sure about disobeying some aspects of the law.

> ¹**Receive one who is weak in the faith,** *but* **not to disputes over doubtful things.** ²**For one believes he may eat all things, but he who is weak eats** *only* **vegetables. (Romans 14:1-2 NKJV)**

The true committed believers must learn to welcome those who are weak in faith. It is natural to be condescending to those who are less confident in their convictions. For the church to be in unity, all must be accepted and co-exist.

God accepted both as they both believe. The weaker in faith must get fully committed in their faith because faith cannot be lukewarm. However. God cannot accept those weak in faith. There are multiple verses in the Scriptures that emphasize this point.

> ²⁴**"No one can serve two masters; for either he will hate the one and love the other, or else he will be loyal to the one and despise the other. You cannot serve God and** [a]**mammon. (Matthew 6:24 NKJV)**

**6** But let him ask in faith, with no doubting, for he who doubts is like a wave of the sea driven and tossed by the wind.

**7** For let not that man suppose that he will receive anything from the Lord;

**8** *he is* a double-minded man, unstable in all his ways. (James 1:6-8 NKJV)

**23** And whatever you do, do it heartily, as to the Lord and not to men,

**24** knowing that from the Lord you will receive the reward of the inheritance; for[a] you serve the Lord Christ. (Colossians 3:23-24 NKJV)

**16** So then, because you are lukewarm, and neither [a]cold nor hot, I will vomit you out of My mouth. (Revelations 3:16 NKJV)

God has accepted both groups. He does not favor one over the other. If God can accept both groups, then Christians, all being saved by God's grace, should accept each other as equals. This also means that they cannot pass judgement on each other. Even though the fully committed in faith know they are free of the law, they must help their fellow members understand with compassion and understanding. Being saved, God has included them into his family and is reluctant to see them as anything else. It is up to the individual to fortify their faith that they are not wavering in their devotion to the Lord. No one lives for themselves, nor do they die for themselves.

Whether a strong believer or weaker in faith, all of us as Christians must remember that we belong to God.

> **3 Let not him who eats despise him who does not eat, and let not him who does not eat judge him who eats; for God has received him.**
>
> **4 Who are you to judge another's servant? To his own master he stands or falls. Indeed, he will be made to stand, for God is able to make him stand.**
>
> **5 One-person esteem *one* day above another; another esteems every day *alike.* Let each be fully convinced in his own mind.**
>
> **6 He who observes the day, observes *it* to the Lord; [a]and he who does not observe the day, to the Lord he does not observe *it.* He who eats, eats to the Lord, for he gives God thanks; and he who does not eat, to the Lord he does not eat, and gives God thanks.**
>
> **7 For none of us lives to himself, and no one dies to himself.**
>
> **8 For if we live, we live to the Lord; and if we die, we die to the Lord. Therefore, whether we live or die, we are the Lord's.**
>
> **9 For to this end Christ died [b]and rose and lived again, that He might be Lord of both the dead and the living. (Romans 14:3-9 NKJV)**

As Paul makes clear, we are in no position to judge another Christian. Only their master can judge them.

**4 Who are you to judge another's servant? To his own master he stands or falls. Indeed, he will be made to stand, for God is able to make him stand. (Romans 14:4 NKJV)**

Yes, there is a judgement day coming. When it comes it will be Jesus who judge all. It is not our place to judge. What we believe has no authority in the judiciousness of God. When we do judge we show contempt for others whether they are believers or non-believers. These types of emotions can become a stumbling block for the believer. None of us are innocent. While we are saved by our faith in Jesus, he will judge all our works and consider which are worthy or worthless. He is our intercessor to God and ultimately, we are held accountable to him.

**10 But why do you judge your brother? Or why do you show contempt for your brother? For we shall all stand before the judgment seat of [c]Christ.**

**11 For it is written:**
**"As I live, says the LORD,**
**Every knee shall bow to Me,**
**And every tongue shall confess to God."**

**12 So then each of us shall give account of himself to God.**

**13 Therefore let us not judge one another [d]anymore, but rather resolve this, not to put a stumbling block or a cause to fall in our brother's way. (Romans 14:10-13 NKJV)**

Yet, there is a freedom for those who are strong believers. This freedom is in the knowledge that we are free from the law. Paul continues to use clean versus unclean food as an analogy for good versus evil. If we are careless and flaunt our freedom over those weaker in faith, it can cause an unintended harm to them. Freedom should be set aside to promote peace, building up the church instead of weakening it. In other words, just because we have freedom doesn't mean it always is acceptable in every instance. A person needs to find their own way. We shouldn't encourage another Christian to contravene their conscious by always exercising our freedom in their presence.  Thus, if one weaker in faith believes something is unclean and cannot consume it, it is in their conscious unclean. Encouraging otherwise is a sin.

**14 I know and am convinced by the Lord Jesus that *there is* nothing unclean of itself; but to him who considers anything to be unclean, to him *it is* unclean.**

**15 Yet if your brother is grieved because of *your* food, you are no longer walking in love. Do not destroy with your food the one for whom Christ died.**

**16 Therefore do not let your good be spoken of as evil;**

**17 for the kingdom of God is not eating and drinking, but righteousness and peace and joy in the Holy Spirit.**

**18 For he who serves Christ in [e]these things *are* acceptable to God and approved by men.**

**19 Therefore let us pursue the things *which make* for peace and the things by which one may [f]edify another.**

**20 Do not destroy the work of God for the sake of food. All things indeed *are* pure, but *it is* evil for the man who eats with [g]offense.**

**21** *It is* good neither to eat meat nor drink wine nor *do anything* by which your brother stumbles [h]or is offended or is made weak.

**22** [i]Do you have faith? Have *it* to yourself before God. Happy *is* he who does not condemn himself in what he approves.

**23** But he who doubts is condemned if he eats, because *he does* not *eat* from faith; for whatever *is* not from faith is [j]sin. (Romans 14:14-23 NKJV)

Having an opinion on what is a sin does not necessarily make it a categorical imperative. The German philosopher Immanuel Kant stated that this is a rule of conduct that is unconditional or absolute for all agents, the validity or claim of which does not depend on any desire or end (Kant, 2010) Basically, he is saying if everybody did the same thing all the time, then the action would most likely be a good action. If the action causes a harm to anyone then it is most likely not a good action.

The Categorical Imperative is a moral compass that only cares about what is right. No matter who the person is or what the person wants the imperative must work for everyone.

The Categorical Imperative includes three formulations:

First Formulation: Act only according to that maxim whereby you can at the same time will that it should become a universal law (Kant,1993).

Second Formulation: Act in such a way that you treat humanity, whether in your own person or in the person of any other, never merely as a means to an end, but always at the same time as an end (Kant,1993).

Third Formulation: Thus, the third practical principle follows [from the first two] as the ultimate condition of their harmony with practical reason: the idea of the will of every rational being as a universally legislating will (Kant,1993).

To paraphrase,

- The Formula of Universality: Act only in a way that you'd be okay with everyone else acting too.

- The Formula of Humanity: Treat others as valuable in themselves, not just as tools to get what you want.

- The Formula of the Kingdom of Ends: Behave like you're making rules for a perfect world where everyone's fair to each other.

In other words, the Categorical Imperative is a moral compass that doesn't care who you are or what you want; it cares about what's right. It's like a universal law for all thinking beings that says, "Do the right thing because it is right, not just when it suits you or when you get rewards."

For the Christian, this means to always to think about the action or thought before executing it. If you would not consider the thought or action good for all then it is probably not a good action. Consider the other person's position and their convictions rather than disparaging them. If disagreements are non-essential convictions and practices, they should be kept to themselves and God. Always error on behalf of the right rather than offend their spiritual brother or sister.

Chapter 14 of this letter is relevant today as it was at the time of the Apostle Paul. Many decisions of the modern Christian are not black or white decisions, and most are non-essential. Using our moral compass and the Word of God we can determine what is a right action.

Sone things are obviously right actions, such as, setting aside love and service to others and be in submission to human authorities. Other actions are bad actions, including sexual immorality, jealousy, drunkenness, or covetousness. But who can define these, God or the law. The believer is free and knows the truth.

# CHAPTER XV

So, who is strong or weak in faith. Should the strong in faith expel the lukewarm. The strong in faith have no fear of the Mosaic laws because they are set free by their faith. The strong in faith are also free of the Jewish traditions e.g. circumcise, animal sacrifice. Jesus came to be the sacrifice for all that believe in him, for all their sins past, present, and future.

We are reminded that Jesus is our example. He did not come to gratify himself or raise himself above others, but he came as a servant placing others ahead of himself. This is how the Christian strong in faith should be to those are weaker in faith. The strong should help the weak. Help them physically when they can. Help them always spiritually with love and compassion. Therefore, all Christians will be of one mind with strong faith in Jesus Christ.

**¹We then who are strong ought to bear with the [a]scruples of the weak, and not to please ourselves.**

**² Let each of us please *his* neighbor for *his* good, leading to [b]edification.**

**³ For even Christ did not please Himself; but as it is written, "The reproaches of those who reproached You fell on Me."**

**⁴ For whatever things were written before were written for our learning, that we through the [c]patience and comfort of the Scriptures might have hope.**

**5** **Now may the God of patience and comfort grant you to be like-minded toward one another, according to Christ Jesus,**

Being of one mind Christians can glorify God together. Jesus came fulfil the promises of God to his people of Israel. He also came to be their servant to show the patience and love of God. But he also came to fulfil the ancient prophecies that foretold the inclusion of Gentiles into his plan and to receive them into his family and to accept their praise as with the converted Jews. Thus, whether Jew or Gentile, all will be believers of Christ and of one mind and voice.

**6** **that you may with one mind *and* one mouth glorify the God and Father of our Lord Jesus Christ.**

**7** **Therefore receive one another, just as Christ also received** [d]**us, to the glory of God.**

**8** **Now I say that Jesus Christ has become a** [e]**servant to the circumcision for the truth of God, to confirm the promises *made* to the fathers,**

**9** **and that the Gentiles might glorify God for *His* mercy, as it is written:**

> **"For this reason, I will confess to You among the Gentiles,
> And sing to Your name."**

**10** **And again he says:**

> **"Rejoice, O Gentiles, with His people!"**

**11** **And again:**

"Praise the LORD, all you Gentiles!
Laud Him, all you peoples!"

**12** And again, Isaiah says:

"There shall be a root of Jesse;
And He who shall rise to reign over the Gentiles,
In Him the Gentiles shall hope." (Romans 15:6-12
NKJV)

Paul then gives a short prayer to the people for their belief. He knows that the Christians in Rome are a good people and righteous in their faith. He explains that for this reason he is more forthright in speaking his mind. He tells them also that it is God that directs him to minister to the Gentiles that they too can share in the Holy Spirit.

**13** Now may the God of hope fill you with all joy and peace in believing, that you may abound in hope by the power of the Holy Spirit.

**14** Now I myself am confident concerning you, my brethren, that you also are full of goodness, filled with all knowledge, able also to admonish [f]one another.

**15** Nevertheless, brethren, I have written more boldly to you on *some* points, as reminding you, because of the grace given to me by God,

**16** that I might be a minister of Jesus Christ to the Gentiles, ministering the gospel of God, that the offering [g]of the Gentiles might be acceptable, sanctified by the Holy Spirit. [(Romans 15:13-16 NKJV)

Peul declares that he has traveled throughout all the nearby regions. He mentions specifically from Jerusalem to Illyricum. He is honored to do the work of the Lord knowing that he is strengthened by the power of Jesus within him.

**¹³ I can do all things through [a]Christ who strengthens me. (Philippians 4:13 NKJV)**

Paul has no power in himself and never claims to have any. He always defers to Jesus and the Holy Spirit for his delivery of the gospel and miracles performed. He was steadfast in his message that salvation is through faith in Christ alone. This he delivered to the people anywhere he traveled. He especially sought out places where people had never heard of Jesus or his message.

**¹⁷ Therefore I have reason to glory in Christ Jesus in the things *which pertain* to God.**

**¹⁸ For I will not dare to speak of any of those things which Christ has not accomplished through me, in word and deed, to make the Gentiles obedient—**

**¹⁹ in mighty signs and wonders, by the power of the Spirit of God, so that from Jerusalem and round about to Illyricum I have fully preached the gospel of Christ.**

**²⁰ And so I have made it my aim to preach the gospel, not where Christ was named, lest I should build on another man's foundation,**

**²¹ but as it is written:**

**"To whom He was not announced, they shall see;
And those who have not heard shall understand."
(Romans 15:17-21 NKJV)**

Regrettably, Paul had never visited Rome in the past. He tells the Christians there that he plans to visit soon as he will go to Rome on his way to Spain. The apostle plans to preach the gospel of Christ to the Gentiles there. Paul wants to expand his missionary journeys since he has traversed the regions in the surrounding areas. As part of his visit to Rome, he hopes to raise funds to help in his missionary work in Spain.

**22 For this reason I also have been much hindered from coming to you.**

**23 But now no longer having a place in these parts, and having a great desire these many years to come to you,**

**24 whenever I journey to Spain, [h]I shall come to you. For I hope to see you on my journey, and to be helped on my way there by you, if first I may enjoy your *company* for a while.**

**25 But now I am going to Jerusalem to [i]minister to the saints.**

**26 For it pleased those from Macedonia and Achaia to make a certain contribution for the poor among the saints who are in Jerusalem.**

**27 It pleased them indeed, and they are their debtors. For if the Gentiles have been partakers of their spiritual things, their duty is also to minister to them in material things.**

**28 Therefore, when I have performed this and have sealed to them this fruit, I shall go by way of you to Spain.**

**29 But I know that when I come to you, I shall come in the fullness of the blessing [j]of the gospel of Christ. (Romans 15:22-29 NKJV)**

Paul tells the church that before he can come to Rome, he must make a trip to Jerusalem to deliver financial aid for the saints there. The Jewish Christians in Jerusalem are very poor and in need of support. They are constantly being ridiculed and disparaged by the Pharisees and Sanhedrin of the traditional Jewish faith. Of course, they were not believers in Jesus as the Messiah. The aid that Paul plans to deliver is from donations collected from Gentile Christians.

Since this journey would be difficult, he asks for the prayers of the church members. The Jewish leaders in Jerusalem know Paul and of his conversion. More importantly, they know of the message he has been delivering about Jesus and how successful he has been in making converts to this new Christian faith. This was a major concern to the religious leaders and social elites since it directly affected their control and power over the people of Israel. It was the mission of the religious leaders of the Jewish to find Paul and kill him. They needed to stop the message of Jesus.

Paul was committed to deliver Jesus's message. This was entrusted to him by Jesus himself. Once he completes this mission, he will be able to visit the Christians in Rome and relax for a time.

**30** Now I beg you, brethren, through the Lord Jesus Christ, and through the love of the Spirit, that you strive together with me in prayers to God for me,

**31** that I may be delivered from those in Judea who [k]do not believe, and that my service for Jerusalem may be acceptable to the saints,

**32** that I may come to you with joy by the will of God, and may be refreshed together with you.

**33** Now the God of peace *be* with you all. Amen. (Romans 15:30-33v NKJV)

# CHAPTER XVI

Paul concludes his letter to the Roman Church. He gives greeting to specific people in Rome and relays greetings from companions and fellow workers in Christ. He mentions Phoebe in particular who receives his letter to deliver to the Roman church. Paul knows Phoebe from a town not far from Corinth.

**¹I commend to you Phoebe our sister, who is a servant of the church in Cenchrea,**

**² that you may receive her in the Lord in a manner worthy of the saints, and assist her in whatever business she has need of you; for indeed she has been a helper of many and of myself also. (Romans 16:1-2 NKJV)**

He then mentions Priscilla and Acquila, a married couple who he spent much time in their nonspiritual work making tents. They became good friends and shared in Paul's ministry. Paul met them in Corinth where they were displaced from Rome as a result of Acquila being a Jew. Emperor Claudius expelled all Jews from Rome and generally it was not safe for Jews in Italy. Priscilla and Acquila helped Paul establish the Corinthian church. Once the ban was lifted, Priscilla and Aquila returned to Rome. Once returned, they established the Christian church in Rome.

**³ Greet Priscilla and Aquila, my fellow workers in Christ Jesus,**

**⁴ who risked their own necks for my life, to whom not only I give thanks, but also all the churches of the Gentiles.**

**5** Likewise *greet* the church that is in their house. Greet my beloved Epaenetus, who is the firstfruits of [a]Achaia to Christ. (Romans 16:3-5 NKJV)

Paul then mentions a myriad of people who we know little about. It appears that they are from various aspects of life. Some are wealthy. Some are poor. Some are Jews. Some are Gentiles. Some are slaves. It seems that they all have a common connection by meeting at the church houses throughout Rome.

**6Greet Mary, who labored much for us.**

**7 Greet Andronicus and Junia, my countrymen and my fellow prisoners, who are of note among the apostles, who also were in Christ before me.**

**8 Greet Amplias, my beloved in the Lord.**

**9 Greet Urbanus, our fellow worker in Christ, and Stachys, my beloved.**

**10 Greet Apelles, approved in Christ. Greet those who are of the *household* of Aristobulus.**

**11 Greet Herodion, my [b]countryman. Greet those who are of the *household* of Narcissus who are in the Lord.**

**12 Greet Tryphena and Tryphosa, who have labored in the Lord. Greet the beloved Persis, who labored much in the Lord.**

**13 Greet Rufus, chosen in the Lord, and his mother and mine.**

**14** Greet Asyncritus, Phlegon, Hermas, Patrobas, Hermes, and the brethren who are with them. **15** Greet Philologus and Julia, Nereus and his sister, and Olympas, and all the saints who are with them.

**16** Greet one another with a holy kiss. [c]the churches of Christ greet you. (Romans 16:6-16 NKJV)

Before Paul concludes his letter, he warns the church members that there are false prophets who will try to poison them. These false prophets will try to cause division with the members by teaching misleading doctrine. The doctrine will be similar to the truth but in reality, it will be counterfeit as some features of their presentation will not be true. He implores the members to stay true to the Lord. Remain obedient and do what is good and God will crush Satan under your feet.

**17** Now I urge you, brethren, note those who cause divisions and offenses, contrary to the doctrine which you learned, and avoid them.

**18** For those who are such do not serve our Lord [d]Jesus Christ, but their own belly, and by smooth words and flattering speech deceive the hearts of the simple.

**19** For your obedience has become known to all. Therefore, I am glad on your behalf; but I want you to be wise in what is good, and [e]simple concerning evil.

**20** And the God of peace will crush Satan under your feet shortly.

The grace of our Lord Jesus Christ *be* with you. Amen. (Romans 16:17-20 NKJV)

He then gives greetings to them from those who were with him in Corinth. He mentions eight in total. All who were companions and fellow workers in Christ.

> **21 Timothy, my fellow worker, and Lucius, Jason, and Sosipater, my countrymen, greet you.**

> **22 I, Tertius, who wrote *this* epistle, greet you in the Lord.**

> **23 Gaius, my host and *the host* of the whole church, greets you. Erastus, the treasurer of the city, greets you, and Quartus, a brother.**

> **24 The[f] grace of our Lord Jesus Christ *be* with you all. Amen. (Romans 16:21-24)**

Paul now ends his letter with praise to God. He tells the members to take heed to what he is telling them. Adhere to his teachings as his authority comes from Jesus. Never forget that with faith we receive God's grace.

> **25 [g]Now to Him who is able to establish you according to my gospel and the preaching of Jesus Christ, according to the revelation of the mystery kept secret since the world began**

> **26 but now made manifest, and by the prophetic Scriptures made known to all nations, according to the commandment of the everlasting God, for obedience to the faith—**

**27** to God, alone wise, *be* glory through Jesus Christ forever. Amen. (Romans 16:25-27 NKJV)

## SUMMARY

The Book of Romans is the longest of the Apostle Paul's epistles. In this letter he provides the theological foundation for anyone to establish their faith in the Lord with understanding of why this is important for salvation. Though he had never been to Rome, Paul was partial to Romans as he was a Roman citizen.

This letter encompasses multiple topics to include original sin, God's sovereignty, judgement, spiritual growth, Jews vs. Gentiles, God's favor, the righteousness of God, and salvation.

Paul stresses the importance of faith in Christ for salvation and the importance of obedience and service to God. He warns of the presence of false prophets that are instruments of Satan who attempt to poison the message of Jesus, God incarnate on Earth. The church members must always remain faithful and supportive of each other in their obedience to God.

Throughout the epistle the righteousness of God is the foundational concept. Only through faith in God's righteousness can salvation be attained.

> **16 For I am not ashamed of the gospel [a]of Christ, for it is the power of God to salvation for everyone who believes, for the Jew first and also for the Greek.**

**17 For in it the righteousness of God is revealed from faith to faith; as it is written, "The just shall live by faith." (Romans 1:16-17 NKJV)**

Paul makes it clear that "good works" is not the way to salvation. We are dead in our sins and only through the grace of God can we be saved. Christians must endeavor to live by a holy regime. We should not conform to the world but live as living sacrifices for God. Only through this standard of living would one lessen their problems in this existence and ensure their happiness in the next.

This letter to the Romans establishes definitively the foundation, the cornerstone of our faith. The foundation is exact. It is established by God and delivered by Jesus. As with any building construction, if the foundation is not exact the building is at risk of catastrophic failure at some time in the future. This is analogous to our spiritual life. We must seek spiritual guidance from the words of Jesus and be aware of any minister or preacher who is not exact in delivering His message.

We also must be aware of any deviation in the future from the declarations of Jesus. Using the building analogy again, if the foundation is solid all additional construction must maintain the same exactness of the foundation. Deviation can cause problems in the future. So to with our spiritual life. We must resist temptation and trust in God to keep us secure with the foundation, which is Jesus.

**13 No temptation has overtaken you except such as is common to man; but God is faithful, who will not allow you to be tempted beyond what you are able, but with the temptation will also make the way of escape, that you may be able to [a]bear it. (I Corinthians 10:13 NKJV)**

Praise be to God who sent Jesus to Saul of Tarsus on the road to Damascus where the most significant conversion from Judaism to the Way occurred. As a result, Saul becomes the Apostle Paul and brings the message of Jesus to the world, Jews and Gentiles.

# Reference

Cross, F. L.; Livingstone, E. A., eds. (2005). "Paul the Apostle". *The Oxford Dictionary of the Christian Church (3rd Revised ed.).* Oxford: Oxford University Press. *pp. 1243–45.* doi:10.1093/acref/9780192802903.001.0001. ISBN 978-0-19-280290-3

Hodges, Frederick M. (2001). "The Ideal Prepuce in Ancient Greece and Rome: Male Genital Aesthetics and Their Relation to Lipodermos, Circumcision, Foreskin Restoration, and the Kynodesme" (PDF). Bulletin of the History of Medicine. **75** (Fall 2001). Johns Hopkins University Press: 375–405. doi:10.1353/bhm.2001.0119. PMID 11568485. S2CID 29580193. Retrieved 3 January 2020.

https://www.merriam.webster.com/dictionary/apostle

https://www.oxfordreference.com/ display/10.1093/oi/authority.20110803095728898

Jacobs, Andrew (2012). Christ Circumcised: A Study in Early Christian History and Difference. United States: University of Pennsylvania Press. ISBN 9780812206517
Stendahl, Krister *(July 1963).* "The Apostle Paul and the Introspective Conscience of the West" (PDF). Harvard Theological Review. *56 (3).* Cambridge: Cambridge University Press *on behalf of the* Harvard Divinity School: *199–215.* doi:10.1017/S0017816000024779. ISSN 1475-4517. JSTOR 1508631. LCCN 09003793. OCLC 803348474. S2CID 170331485. Archived (PDF) *from the original on 24 December 2021.* Retrieved 12 February 2022.

# Bibliography

Bokenkotter, Thomas (2004). A Concise History of the Catholic Church (Revised and expanded ed.). Doubleday. pp. 19–21. ISBN 0-385-50584-1.

Dunn, James D. G., ed. (2003), The Cambridge Companion to St. Paul, Cambridge: Cambridge University Press, *ISBN 0-521-78155-8*

Kant, Immanuel *(1993) [1785].* Groundwork of the Metaphysics of Morals. Translated by Ellington, James W. (3rd ed.). Hackett. p. 30. ISBN 0-87220-166-X. It is standard to also reference the Akademie Ausgabe of Kant's works. The Groundwork occurs in the fourth volume. Citations throughout this article follow the format 4: x. For example, the above citation is taken from 4:421.

Ibid, p. 36. 4:429.

Ibid, p. 43. 4:431

Israel Drazi (2009). Maimonides and the Biblical Prophets. Gefen Publishing House Ltd. p. 209.

www.ingramcontent.com/pod-product-compliance
Lightning Source LLC
Chambersburg PA
CBHW081337120626
46546CB00011B/3382